From There to Here

A Family Memoir

By

Donna (Fasone) Blaha

DJFB Publishing
Wimauma, FL

This is my memoir of growing up on the west side of Chicago in an Italian American family in the 1950s and 1960s. The people are real, but names and places are fictitious.

Acknowledgment

I wish to acknowledge and thank my family members, living and deceased, for the laughs, tears, anger, and forgiveness, and the resultant lessons learned. I also wish to thank Arlene Miller for her support and advice.

Part I

I wrote this memoir 50 years ago. I then stuck it in a box and forgot about it. It's a story about growing up in an Italian American Catholic family in a blue-collar neighborhood in Chicago. This story takes place in the 1950s and 1960s.

My family lived on the west side of Chicago. My parents were both children of immigrants. Mom was a homemaker and Dad was a peddler. Unfortunately, both came from poor families. Mom was able to attend 2 years of high school before she had to find a job; while dad had to leave school in 3rd grade to work as a peddler with his parents.

We never did much together as a family. No family vacations or anything like that. For me, the big event of the week was the Sunday dinner with relatives. There was a lot of great food: antipasto, chicken, pasta, eggplant, and on and on. We all were substantial eaters as it was a cultural thing in our family. If you didn't eat well, you insulted the cook.

In addition to eating, there was fun. My cousin, Gino Jr., and I would poke and tickle each other at the table to irritate Gino Sr. He'd explode in a fit of rage at the ruckus from Gino Jr. and me. Gino Jr. and I would laugh at the explosions of broken English and various Italian cuss words. As I look back, the senior family members are no longer with us, and now Gino and I are the seniors.

The Sunday dinners were held in our place or at one of my mother's sister's homes. The oldest sister, Rose, married Gino Ricci (Gino Sr.). Gino Jr. was their son, and Maria was their daughter. Maria was older than Gino Jr. and moved out of state after high school for a job opportunity. Aunt Rose, like all of her sisters, was approximately 5 feet tall. When Aunt Rose's hair began to gray, she dyed it red for, in her words, a 'natural' look. Aunt Rose was

round-faced, good-natured, and loved a good martini. She always spoke her mind and was a great storyteller.

Uncle Gino left Italy by stowing away on a ship when he was a teenager. He spoke English with a very heavy Italian accent. When he arrived in America, he spoke no English, but he learned quickly and was always able to find work to support himself. Uncle Gino was partially bald and wore dark-rimmed glasses. A strict Catholic, he faithfully followed the Pope and spoke of the old country with reverence.

Mom's other two sisters, Carmella and Camille were born 11 months apart. They lived together and worked in the same garment factory. They were so much alike that we often regarded them as one unit. We referred to them as "the aunts." Both were dark-haired, large-nosed, and gregarious. They often spoke simultaneously. Nobody could understand how they did this. My mother, Grace, was the youngest. She, too, dyed her hair red for some reason. Mom was short and overweight. She was the quietest of the bunch. I do not know if it was by choice or because her older sisters were so boisterous and chatty.

My father, Tony, was loud and uncouth. This is because he had minimal education and grew up on rough streets. Tony was born at the turn of the 20th century and peddled fruits and vegetables from a horse and buggy. He was the family's odd one out because he refused to attend Mass and was Sicilian. This was not favorably looked upon by my

mom's Italian family.

Chapter One

In the 50s, we lived on the first floor of a red brick 2-flat building on Chicago's west side. The aunts lived on the second floor, and Aunt Rose and Uncle Gino lived in a wooden bungalow next door. This neighborhood was primarily Italian with a sprinkling of nearby Mexican families. It was often a saint's feast day and that meant long processions of elderly Italian women marching down the street carrying a large, decorated statue. The processions were fun for the kids who dressed in Sunday best and ran up and down the streets causing mischief.

Neighborhoods were quite segregated then due to the influx of European immigrants during the industrial revolution. Because most could not speak English, they lived in areas where they could converse with their neighbors. Remnants of the former residents remain. You might find a great ethnic restaurant in one of the old Chicago neighborhoods, but the people are long gone.

We didn't need a telephone in those days. If mom needed to reach the aunts upstairs, she'd bang on the radiator, and they'd hear the signal upstairs and walk to the staircase so they could chat there. If we needed to speak to Aunt Rose, we opened a window and tapped on one of her windows. (Houses were built remarkably close.) Mom and Aunt Rose would sit on their windowsills and chat via window for hours on a lovely day.

It was a typical Sunday morning, and my parents were fighting. I could hear them as I lay in bed. I had no idea what the fight was about as they were yelling in Italian. They refused to teach us their first language so they could fight in a language I could not understand.

One day I asked mom if I could go next door and play with Gino Jr. We, except dad, attended the early Mass, and I had nothing to do after church. My sister was 4 years younger, and that was a big age difference at that time in our lives. When I approached Aunt Rose's front door, Francesca, the elderly woman next door, who was usually peering from behind her front window curtains, quickly opened her window and threw a pan of water at my head. Honestly, I think she had nothing better to do. I do know she did not like my father because he parked his truck in front of her house when it was the only available parking space on our street.

Francesa, with her white hair, pulled back into a tight bun, shouted "you tell-a you papa no to park his-a truck over here. He cut-a oxygen off from my window." She then slammed her window shut.

When Aunt Rose came to the door she asked if I had just taken a bath. "No," I said. "It was Francesa again."

 She understood. "Come on in, Josie," she said.

Aunt Rose was wearing a bathrobe held closed by two large safety pins. Her hair was in curlers, and she wore pink, well-worn slippers. I was crazy about her. She had so much personality, while my mom and aunts were always well-groomed and neatly dressed.

Aunt Rose shouted, "Hey Gino, Josie's here!"

Gino came running up the stairs from the basement. "I was down in the basement playing with my electric train. Come on down, Josie." I ran down the basement stairs after him.

"How's tricks, Gino?"

"Oh, not good," Gino said.

I asked him what was wrong. "Well, you know Sister Rafaela, my homeroom teacher?"

"Yes," I said.

"I was talking in class, and she threw a bottle of ink at me. I ducked and it hit Frankie Salerno in the head! Sister Rafaela grabbed me by the cheek and took me down to the principal's office. She said I'll be sent to Lutheran School if I get into any further trouble."

"Lutheran School," I gasped! "Those people go to hell. They aren't Catholics!" I felt sorry for Gino. He was worried.

I liked Gino's train set and playing together, but I did not like his friends. One day, his friend, Jimmy Scardino, saw me walking to school in the rain and grabbed my umbrella, and ran off with it. When I got to school, I was wet and crying. My teacher, Sister Philippa, made me stand in the corner for acting like a baby. I did not like another one of Gino's friends either. His name was Rocky Serritella. He wrote harsh words in my notebook and when Sister Philippa saw them, I was banished to detention after school. Rocky wrote 'menstruation' in my notebook. When I asked him what it was, he said it was a beautiful flower. Gino and his friends were a few years older than me and made fun of me, but Gino never did.

It was time for me to return home. The aunts were in the kitchen helping mom prepare the dinner. Aunt Rose, Uncle Gino, and Gino Jr. were due to come to our house for Sunday dinner.

Soon we would all be sitting around our large dining room table. I set out the plates and cutlery. The aunts prepared the salad and mom managed the main course and dessert. Uncle Gino and Dad sat in the living room and drank shots of whiskey and Budweiser beer. Mom and the aunts rarely touched hard liquor. They did drink red wine with dinner though. During Lent, we had a meatless meal: homemade cavatelli with marinara sauce and a side dish of zucchini. Salad and Italian bread were always on the table. Aunt Rose asked if we all received our ashes on Ash Wednesday. Everyone nodded.

"We had Father Angelo," said Aunt Camille.

"Well, you're lucky," said Aunt Rose. "I had Father Coco, and this is the last year he's getting ashes in my eyes! I could hardly see when I left the altar rail. He does it every single year – on purpose."

"Rose," Uncle Gino reprimanded. "He no put-a ashes in my face, Rose. You imagine this."

"Listen, Buster," Rose said. "He does this every year. He doesn't like me because I fight with him in the Confessional."

"Why you-a fight, Rose," asked Uncle Gino.

"Because I confessed to using birth control, and he said I'm going to hell. So, I said, I'll see you there, padre!"

"Sacrilege!" shouted Uncle Gino. He did not like any criticism of the clergy or the church.

Aunt Carmella tossed the salad and Mom proclaimed, "Dinner's ready."

Dad put Italian records on our record player, and we listened to Italian love songs during our meal. That is when the argument started.

"Eat more pasta, Josie," and you will live to be a hundred.

That was Aunt Carmella. At that point, Aunt Camille said that eating the skin on the chicken was the key to longevity.

"I said it was the pasta," confirmed Aunt Carmella.

"No, it was the chicken skin," shouted Camille. "You're a know-it-all."

"So are you." "You shut up!" "No, you shut up!"

"Everybody shut up!" shouted Uncle Gino. "Ma Jesu!"

The rest of us calmly ate our dinner as the aunts sneered at each other throughout the rest of the meal.

"You know," said Aunt Rose. "I'm right about Father Coco. Remember last Christmas when we had to kneel at the altar rail to kiss the feet of the Bebe Jesu? Well, Coco slammed that porcelain statue into my mouth and chipped my front tooth. I should have sent him my dental bill. He does these things on purpose."

"It was an accident, Rose, "said my mother. "A priest wouldn't deliberately try to injure you."

"Never mind," said Aunt Rose. "Priests and nuns act holy, but they are just people. Remember this, Josie," said Aunt Rose. "Watch out for those who act holy in this life; they are the biggest sinners!"

"Shut-a you mouth and eat," shouted Uncle Gino. "No more sacrilege!"

My mom, ignoring the whole conversation, brought dessert to the table – a bowl of fresh fruit, nuts, nutcrackers, and a plate of cannolis.

Chapter Two

It was Christmas Eve and the family gathered at Uncle Gino and Aunt Rose's house for dinner. As is the tradition, this was a meatless meal. We dined on calamari, smelts, oysters, clams, and other fishes. Aunt Rose told the story of the fluorescent light burning out in the bathroom. Uncle Gino asked Gino Jr. to go to the Hardware Store and ask for a star. (This was Uncle Gino's pronunciation of the word "starter.")

When Gino asked the hardware manager for a star, the manager apologized, "We're out of stars; would you like an angel?"

So, that day, Gino Jr. brought home an angel tree topper. Aunt Rose laughed, with cannoli oozing out of the corner of her mouth. Uncle Gino scolded Gino Jr. Aunt Rose defended her son, "How was he to know you meant starter for a fluorescent light, Gino?"

Crack, crack, crack! That was me, cracking my knuckles. The aunts jumped.

"Don't do that, Josie or your fingers will become deformed, and nobody will ever marry you." "Oh, leave her alone." Aunt Rose came to my defense. "You're so bossy, Camille, said Carmella. It's obvious why you never married."

"Oh, I had opportunities, Rose. Remember Nicky Lorenzo? He wanted to marry me."

"He was a greasy D.P.," chimed Rose." and his mother was a whore. You know the whole family had poor health."

"You're wrong," retorted Camille. "He was a good, hard, worker."

"It's a good thing you didn't marry into that sickly family," reminded Rose. "Your kids would have been sick all the time. Good thing Nicky died."

"Ah, marriage is-a wonderful-a thing," Uncle Gino said. When-a Rose and I marry, we go to Indiana for honey-a-moon, and she meet all-a my cousins."

Rose had a blank look on her face.

"Who cares?" asked Rose, as she lit a cigarette.

Uncle Gino never approved of his wife's smoking. A few weeks earlier, she bummed a cigarette from her cousin, Antoinette, and liked it. Uncle Gino scowled but Aunt Rose just continued to puff and told him to mind his own business.

Gino and I cleared the plates from the table while Dad and Uncle Gino went into the living room to watch TV.

"Hey, Grace, tell the family about what happened when Father Angelo came to bless the houses last week." Mom blushed but went ahead to tell her story.

As it turns out, mom was hanging clothes on the clothesline in the basement when the doorbell rang. I opened the door (which I was never supposed to do without yelling, "Who is it?")

"Mama, there's a man at the door for you," I shouted down the basement stairs. Mama started cussing up a storm!

"Damn it, Josie! I told you to never open the door to strangers."

She ran up the stairs and saw the poor young priest standing at the door.

"Excuse me, but I'm Father Angelo. I came to bless your house." (As if it would do any good.)

The young, embarrassed priest blessed our house and then left to bless the house next door, Aunt Rose's house. Same scenario. Gino opened the door and called out to his mom.

"Mama, there's a man at the door."

Aunt Rose, in her bathrobe and curled hair, perturbed, shouted, "Damn it and son of a bee, Gino! How many times did I tell you to not open the door to strangers? Wait 'til I tell your father what you did!"

Aunt Rose promptly asked the priest to identify himself.

"I'm Father Angelo and I came to bless your house. You're Catholic, right?"

"Yeh, yeh. We are. Say, have you been to my sister's house next door?"

"Yes," said the priest, "I see the resemblance."

Father Angelo must have wondered about the good Catholic families in our neighborhood. Mama said she was embarrassed to cuss in front of the clergy, but Aunt Rose said it was a good education for the young priest.

Chapter Three

The Easter season was both good and bad. It was good because Catholics could give up Lenten fasting and go back to having fun. Like most kids, I gave up candy for my Lenten sacrifice. This was important for a kid. The adults could not eat in between meals during Lent, so Easter Sunday was a day when adults ate like pigs and kids stuffed their mouths with candy. On Easter Sunday, the family celebrated at Camille and Carmella's apartment. It was a day Uncle Gino drove us crazy with tradition.

The day started with brunch. This consisted of shots of brandy with coffee, eggs, and calzones. Calzones are Italian loaves of bread stuffed with crumbled sausage meat, eggs, parsley, and various kinds of cheese. They are heavenly. Afterward, Uncle Gino insisted we listen to Cavalleria Rusticana, an Italian opera We had to remain silent. This was torture for Gino and me. The adults loved this stuff and, honestly, to this day I cannot stand opera. I overdosed on it as a kid. Gino and I preferred to listen to Fats Domino, Buddy Holly, or Chuck Berry. Another issue we had with it is that we could not understand it. It was in Italian, and we had to remain silent and listen to what we did not understand. It was torture.

Another semi-annual tradition was Uncle Gino reading the letter from his sister who lived in Potenza, Italy. Of course, the letter was long and very boring. We could not understand a word of it, and when he translated it, it was still boring. It seemed there was not much happening in Potenza.

One night, another bombshell dropped. Aunt Rose and Uncle Gino had two cousins over. Each had a martini to drink.

Then Aunt Rose blurted out, "but we ate the olives in the martinis after midnight! We forgot all about it and received communion the next morning at Mass."

(In the 1950s, the Catholic Church forbade the consumption of any food after midnight if Communion was to be received the next day.)

Mama looked shocked. "Did you go to Confession yet?"

"Well, yes," said Aunt Rose, but the next day I purposely stood in line for Father Angelo's confession because you know I can't stand that bastard, Coco!"

"Watch-a you language, Rose!" reprimanded Uncle Gino.

"Anyway," Rose continued, "Father Angelo said no sin was committed because it wasn't intentional. It was an accident, and all was well. He is a nice young man. Thank God I can avoid Father Coco from now on."

"Aunt Rose," I inquired, "Do you think God would send you to hell for eating an olive anyway? I mean it seems unfair to be in hell with Nazis and other murderers because you ate an olive."

"Just listen to the priests," Uncle Gino responded. I never did understand the rules of our religion.

My father walked into the room, and he was in a bad mood because his team, the White Sox, had lost a game. He stalked out the door. The family was upset because he left the house on a religious holiday, not because he cared one way or the other. The Sox were far more important to him. Mama was upset and wanted to go after him.

"Leave him be," scolded Carmella. Then she turned toward Rose and said, "I see you have another martini in your hand, Rose!"

"Aunt Rose said, "Where do you want me to put my drink? In my foot?" She laughed a hoarse laugh and took another drag on her cigarette.

Chapter Four

Italian weddings were always fun. Dominick DeFrancisco's wedding was one of them.
His mom, Angie, was a good family friend. She grew up next to my mother's family on
Taylor Street in Chicago. Today this area is known as Little Italy as this is where the
Italian immigrants settled when they arrived in Chicago. Dominick had been discharged
from the army and was marrying Linda Cairo, a beautician. The wedding couple was both
short and chubby. The reception took place in an event space in the neighborhood. The
bride wore a tiered lace dress that made her look 2 feet wider than she already was. Her
hairdo was a foot tall which was the style at that time. Her eye makeup consisted of two
thick black lines on her lids, and her smile was punctuated by dimpled cheeks.

We all walked up to the receiving line, kissed the bride and groom, and handed the happy
couple 'the envelope' which the bride placed in a white satin bag. The custom is to give
money at a wedding. I heard Angie tell Dominick she wanted a list of guests and the total
of their monetary gifts within a week. That was another custom, I believe.

Anyway, Gino Jr. ran around the dance floor, and I walked around checking the place and
the people out. Next to our table sat the DelVecchio sisters. Together they weighed about
600 pounds. The sisters had never married, and I never asked why. With them sat
Francine Scandura. She, too, was very overweight. Francine was sad because her husband
had left her. Alfredo married her so he could more easily become a citizen. Everyone
cried when he left because he stole all of their money and rejoined another family he had
in Italy. We were horrified! Francine said she'd kill him if she ever laid eyes on him
again, but that didn't happen, so she sat at the table and cried into her wine. She was only

29 but looked much older. Francine had an extremely large bust that stuck straight out. I often thought of it as a shelf where she could place her wine glass.

Mama's cousin Tessie and her husband, Joe, flew in from Florida. Aunt Rose jumped up to give them a big kiss.

"Hey, Tessie!" she called when they entered the reception hall.

They were nice people. Uncle Gino poured Bardolino into everyone's wine glass. Gino and I were allowed to drink 7-Up mixed with a tiny bit of wine. Our drink looked like a pink spritzer and was quite tasty. Tessie asked me if I remembered her. Dumb question, I thought, since the last time I saw her, I was 18 months of age.

Dad chimed in, always the spoiler. "I wouldn't give you two cents for a Florida grapefruit."

Everything in his mind was related to fruits and vegetables.

Tessie said, "I see you're still in the produce business, Tony."

Tessie smiled. A real lady!

When the aunts walked into the room, Tessie said, "You remember Grace and Rose's sisters, right, Joe?"

"No," Joe flatly said with a blank look.

He was bored, and now I understand why. He was the superintendent of schools in Miami. His wife's family was putting him into a coma with their conversation.

Dad returned to his fruit topic, "How can you stand Florida? It's hot, but it is good for tropical fruits. You folks grow fruits?"

"No," said Joe. "We live in the city."

Then Uncle Gino started listing all the vegetables and herbs he grew in his backyard in the city. Joe was completely disinterested.

"Enough vegetation," said Rose, waving her arms. "Let's move on."

I decided to walk around and to find Gino Jr. He was at the sweet table. It was full of cream puffs, honey balls, sesame cookies, and other delightful treats. We both grabbed some of the goodies and then headed to the table as the waiters brought the food out. I filled up a plate with gooey sweets and placed it on a chair to save my place at the table Gino and I selected. I walked back to the family table to grab a plate my mother had filled with pasta and salad. At that time, Sal Indovino absent-mindedly plopped himself on top of my plate of gooey desserts. Sal had a massive rear end and had no idea what was attached to his backside. I was nervous, but Gino laughed hysterically.

"Eh, Gino," Uncle Gino queried, "Why you-a laugh?"

"Oh, nothing, dad. Something just struck me as funny."

"Stop-a the funny business and sit and eat with la famiglia."

Thus, Gino headed back to the parents' table. Sal and his wife, Philomena Luigia, were both very large people. I rued the time that Sal would stand up with my plate of desserts glued to his rear. I will be murdered, I thought, if they find out I left that dessert on that chair. In the meantime, we all enjoyed watching the DelVecchio sisters and Francine eat because they seemed to savor each morsel of food with sheer happiness. Their dimples moved in and out like little accordions as they chewed.

Sal was wearing a maroon-colored suit with a flowered shirt. Philomena Luigia wore a purple brocade dress. I kept watching Sal out of the corner of my eye.

"Mangia," Uncle Gino commanded. I had lost my appetite out of fear and poked at my pasta.

"Nobody will marry you if you-a too skinny. Eat-a Josie, Mangia!" Uncle Gino reprimanded.

The aunts chatted away with Tessie. Joe sat there, bored. Papa sipped his wine and probably pondered the price of Florida citrus.

"I'm-a full," said Uncle Gino. He let out a huge burp.

"Pig," Aunt Rose drolly said.

"You 'gotta no good manners, Rose!"

Uncle Gino explained that it's complimentary to burp after a good meal. This was an Italian custom that Aunt Rose never liked. I left the table to get a plate of sweets. Gino Jr. and I stared at Sal. When he stood up, the cannoli cream was starting to ooze from his behind. My plate of sweets was still firmly attached to his backside. As Sal walked across the dance floor, my ooey-gooey plate slowly slide down to the top of his legs. Guests started to point and laugh at the enormity of the mess. When Philomena saw what caused all the laughter, she jumped to her feet and ran after her husband.

"Sal! Sal! Oh, mama mia, mama mia!"

Playing dumb, Gino and I calmly walked back to our table with the desserts.

"What's going on, Josie?" I played dumb.

"I don't know, mom."

Inside, I was afraid they'd somehow know it was my dessert plate affixed to Sal'a behind. Sal hurried to the men's room, Philomena scurrying behind him.

"Hey, look at fat Sal," shouted my father, "What an ass!"

Papa was having a good belly laugh.

Mama said, "Let's go home, Tony. Josie looks white. She must be coming down with something."

"Yes, I don't feel good," I confirmed, eager to get out of there.

"Take care of yourself," chimed the aunts in unison.

Papa was looped. Mama didn't like when he drove drunk.

"You know I don't like when you drive like this, Tony!"

"Well, learn how to drive then," he said.

Papa was driving in the wrong direction. Mama was beside herself with anger.

"Tony, you're driving the wrong way!" she shouted.

Papa said, "It's the tires; I'm going to get some of those new sibling tires. I hear they are the best."

The ride seemed to last an eternity. It was a few blocks from our home, yet the circuitous

ride took about 40 minutes. I was grateful when we were home and away from the

DeFrancisco wedding.

Chapter Five

By summer, Gino and I weren't playing together very much. Our neighborhood was racially changing. There were racial outbursts and fights. Mom walked me to school each day. Dad spent his free time at the racetrack or watching the White Sox on TV. Mama watched her soap operas in the kitchen.

"Hey, Grace!" Dad yelled. "Look at that jag-off they just put on first base. Goddam Sox are no good anymore."

Mama ignored him.

"And they put that son-of-a-bitch up to bat!"

"Tony, please, clean up your mouth! Josie's in the house."

"Run, run you bastard! Run! Wait."

"Josie, go next door!" Mama had enough of my father's foul language.

I approached Aunt Rose's house very carefully, certain that old lady Francesca wasn't at her window. I wasn't in the mood for a shower.

"Come in, Josie, and stay for lunch."

So, I accepted Aunt Rose's invitation and then went into Gino's bedroom. He was jumping on the bed, and I joined him.

"Close the door, Josie. Mama doesn't like it when I jump on the bed."

We were bored with jumping after a few minutes. Gino Jr. then told me a story. This morning, my dad's co-worker, Emil, called and asked him to come into the restaurant where he worked. In the meantime, I told mama that if Benny Rizzo comes to the door, tell him I don't want to play. Mama said OK. A short time after that, Emil showed up at the door. Mama opened the door. Emil asked if Gino was home.

"Thinking he must be Benny, mama said, 'Gino can't come out to play, he's babysitting for his Aunt Grace.' Wait! There's more," giggled Gino Jr. Emil thought my mom was a nut or something, so he phoned my dad to see what was going on.

Dad was mad at mama, but she responded, "It's your fault! I didn't want two Ginos in the same house. I wanted to name him Nick!"

"Your mom is funny, Gino!" I laughed.

"Yes, she is. The two of them are like the comedy hour."

Aunt Rose heated some leftover braciola, and it was delicious. They are thin pieces of flank steak stuffed with breadcrumbs, cheese, and herbs. They are then tied with string and simmered in a red sauce. I told Aunt Rose my mom made braciola a few weeks ago, but dad wouldn't eat them. He couldn't find the strings and accused my mom of using dissolving rubber bands to secure them. It was ridiculous.

Aunt Rose shook her head, "Your dad can be a dumb ass."

"I know, Aunt Rose.

Years ago, a fortune-teller told him he'd die from food poisoning, so he is very fussy about food. He has accused my mom of poisoning him on various occasions.

Aunt Rose said, "What a jerk! I told your mom to never marry a Sicilian, so what does she come home with? I know he's your father and you should respect him for that, Josie, but your mom could have done better." Rose continued, "In life, you make your bed, then you sleep in it."

I thanked Aunt Rose for the lunch. She blushed.

"You know your Uncle Gino's a good cook, too."

"Yes, I said. He was a bachelor for a while and learned to prepare delicious food."

My aunts popped in wearing pedal pushers and nice blouses. Aunt Carmella was a cracker jack tailor and sewed most of their clothes and ours. Mama never had enough money to buy us clothes, and we wore uniforms to Catholic School. Everything else was made by Aunt Carmella. Aunt Rose took the percolator off of the stove and poured coffee for the aunts. My entire family was heavy-duty coffee drinkers.

Aunt Camille pushed my bangs out of my eyes. I didn't like when she did that.

"Leave my bangs be, please," I pleaded.

"Leave her alone," said Rose.

Camille said, "You always side with the kids, Rose!"

"Because you're always wrong!" shouted Rose. She continued, "You'd get more accomplished in life if you kept your big mouth shut. So, if her bangs bother her, she'll eventually cut them." At that point, Gino and I said goodbye to everyone and ran down into the basement to play a board game.

Part Two

Introduction

Things changed considerably in the 1960s. The Italian families moved away, and our old neighborhood turned into a crime-infested slum. Uncle Gino and Aunt Rose moved to the northside of Chicago, and we moved further west, into a predominantly Irish neighborhood. My parents bought another two-flat, and my two aunts moved upstairs. This neighborhood was strange to me at first. The people weren't as friendly. I was an odd ball in a classroom full of O'Connors, Gallaghers, and McNamaras. The priests and nuns couldn't pronounce my surname, and I looked different in a sea of freckled redheads and blue-eyed blondes, and fair-skinned brunettes. The only consolation was that old lady Francesca wouldn't be dousing me with water any longer. I was older now and wanted to meet some new friends.

My father was still anti-church. He didn't like the Irish church or anyone very much and had no friends. I was in high school now. We had some new family members – three alley cats that we adopted. The pets became mama's babies, and I became more independent. Uncle Gino and Aunt Rose adopted a pet, too, a bird that spoke Italian. Our cats ate cat food, but they also ate leftovers, like rigatoni and meatballs. It's no wonder they were overweight– they were Italian cats!

Colleen and Beth were my best friends in high school. I met them in various classes. We were the products of K through 12 Catholic education. That means we were naïve. We rarely went out with boys because our high school was all girls, and our nuns were very strict. We were pretty content, and ignorance was bliss. For dances, we'd ask a friend's

28

brother, and the nuns preferred that the boy was from a neighborhood Catholic boy's school. Our lives consisted of school, homework, bowling club, and Friday night pizza and Coca-Cola parties. We put on our Beatle albums and danced together.

One day, I ran down our front steps and noticed the old man next door. Mr. Leone (a rare Italian in my neighborhood) sat quietly. I greeted him and smiled. As I walked past his house, a stream of water made me jump.

"Hey," I yelled.

He scowled and called me something in Italian.

"Leave me alone!" I yelled.

Then I felt bad that I said that and realized I'd better go to confession if I planned to receive Communion at Sunday mass. I was on my way to a bowling alley on Madison Street, one block away. Always the introspective child, I pondered my life. Was I happy? Yes. I liked my friends, had a good record collection, and I was doing very well in school. Then – a negative thought entered my mind. I had no boyfriend like the public-school girls. Well, I consoled myself with the thought that my grades were good, I was planning to go to college and boyfriends could wait.

It was Wednesday and that was the day we bowled after school. Colleen and Beth were on my team. I served as the secretary of my school's bowling team. I liked the job because I computed all of the girls' averages and handicaps. As secretary, I was in the know on the stats!   The owner of "Westside Bowl" chewed on a fat, wet cigar and handed us a scoresheet. We laced up our shoes, bowling bags in hand, and headed to our assigned lanes. Some cute boys were bowling in the lane next to ours. They looked our age – 15 or 16.

"Hey, do you think they go to Catholic School?" queried Beth.

"Don't stare, Beth. We'll look desperate." I chided.

I couldn't help but notice a blonde boy with a crew cut. He was about 5' 6" tall and wore a red and black, short-sleeved shirt with black trousers. His pal called him "John." The boy next to him resembled him but was chubbier. They had to be brothers.

"Hurry up, Josie; it's your turn."

I needed to stop looking at the blonde boy and focus on my game. I rolled a spare. Colleen was an excellent bowler and had already rolled 2 strikes in a row. At this time, Beth noted that the boys were looking our way.

"Which one do you like," asked Beth.

I smiled at the blonde boy and said, "I like the crew cut."

"Figures," said Beth. "I guess I get the chubby one."

At that point, John (crew cut) walked our way and approached me. Colleen blushed. I froze. A lump swelled in my throat.

"Hi," said John. "I'm John Kozlowski."

I smiled and introduced myself. "Hi, I'm Josie Lorenzo."

John said he and his brother would like to buy us cokes. Colleen and Beth hurried over, foaming at the mouth with enthusiasm.

After a hasty introduction, they both said, 'Sure!"

John introduced the chubby boy as his brother, Stan. The handsome, dark-haired boy was Paul Fanone. Stan then went to the refreshment stand and returned with 6 bottles of Coke. We thanked the boys and asked where they went to school.

"We go to St. Michael's," said Paul.

St. Michael's was about a mile away from the bowling alley. Most families in that area were Polish, like John and Stan.

"Gee, that's not too far from where we live," gushed Colleen.

Paul and Colleen seemed to hit it off and were chattering away. Stan and Beth were conversing also.

"Would you like to go to a dance with us sometime?" asked John.

I couldn't believe John asked me out to a school dance! My first dance! Colleen and Beth were approached, too, and we were all in seventh heaven.

When the games were over, John offered to walk me home, but I told him I lived too far away and had to take the bus home. He understood. So, we exchanged phone numbers, and I rode the bus home in a trance. I guess we're all set, mumbled Beth. She wasn't enthusiastic about Stan but was grateful for her first date. I was excited beyond belief. To date, the only boy I'd ever been friends with was Frank Torti. I knew him from the neighborhood, and we'd hang out together at times, but we were just friends.

Later that night, John phoned me at home. I found out that he was 17, and Stan was 16. They were born in Poland but came to the U.S. as babies. Their parents didn't speak English, and the boys were bilingual.

"I'd like you to meet my folks, Josie, but don't tell them you're not Polish right away. They are fussy about that sort of thing."

"Oh, I understand, John," I said. "My parents are the same way about dating Italians, but you'll meet my parents, too. It'll be an interesting experience."

The following Saturday, John came to pick me up after school so we could go to a movie together. My parents weren't home, so I felt a sense of relief because I knew they'd look at him and know immediately that he was not Italian. Anyway, the theater was about a block away on Madison Street. I can't remember what we saw, but it was exciting to be on a date. When John walked me home, we paused at the door. He leaned forward to kiss me, and I went into a state of panic. I had never been kissed before. What should I do? Pucker up? Play dumb and quickly open the door? I was scared!

"Uh, um, I can't kiss you, John," I blurted out.

"Why not?" he looked astonished.

"Well, I just met you and, you know. I'm Catholic." John looked surprised.

"I'm Catholic, too! So what?"

I responded, "Um, I think you're supposed to know a person better before you do any of that stuff."

"That's ridiculous, Josie," he scoffed. "Do you believe all that stuff the nuns and priests tell you? They are all freaks!"

I was stunned by John's sacrilege, calling nuns and priests freaks.

"OK, OK," he said. "I get it."

John then turned around and said, "Talk to you later, OK?"

"OK," I responded.

I ran into the house, crying. I knew he'd never call, and he didn't. I felt so awkward.

That next Sunday, Gino Jr. and his parents drove to our house. Mama was in the basement. She was often in the basement since she started her 'change of life.' We didn't have air conditioning, and the basement was cooler. I had set the dinner table and couldn't wait for the family to arrive. It would take my mind off the fact that I blew it on my first date.

"Go stir the sauce, Josie," mama yelled from the basement.

"OK," I replied.

Dad was in the living room reading the Chicago Tribune.

"Damn horse-racin'," he muttered. "Can't get it out of my blood. It's poison."

"Hey, dad," I said, "Would you get some beer from the back porch? The family is coming over."

"Yea, he said," I'll put the beer in the fridge."

While my father tended to the beer, the doorbell rang. It was the aunts. They had the key, so they walked into the house. They reluctantly greeted my father. They disliked my father, and the feeling was mutual.

"Josie," dad barked, "Go get your mother in the basement."

"Will do," I confirmed.

I greeted my aunts.

"My we look pretty today, Josie," Aunt Camille said, smiling.

"Thanks," I retorted.

The aunts always looked younger than their years. They had a few gray hairs but always dressed neatly and ate a healthy diet. Much like our diet, it was heavy in pasta, vegetables, and fruit.

"You look nice, too," I responded.

"We look nice because we were never married," said Aunt Carmella.

"I hope your mother gets through her change of life soon," said Camille. "She's in the basement too often."

Soon, Aunt Rose, Uncle Gino, and Gino Jr. arrived. Gino was older now. He had graduated high school and was working at an electronics store. Dad and Uncle Gino enjoyed their beer, and Aunt Rose enjoyed a martini with a cigarette. Back in the 1960s and even beyond, people smoked in their houses. I couldn't stand the smell, and I was sneezing and blowing my nose a lot. The doctor confirmed that I had allergies. Aunt

Camille asked what the doctor said about my allergies, and I told her wanted me to take some pills and get weekly allergy shots.

Aunt Carmella said, "Josie if you think positively, your allergies will go away. You can heal yourself."

I shook my head negatively and said nothing had worked for me, so I was going to start the allergy shot program.

"Make a novena and go light a candle in the church," said Aunt Camille. "That will make you heal. You don't need to make a doctor rich with his allergy shots."

Aunt Carmella asked me if the problem was nerves.

"Is school bothering you?" asked Aunt Rose.

"No, no," I protested. "I like school."

"I bet it's nerves," confirmed Rose.

"I'm NOT nervous!" I screamed.

Once again, I was told to light a candle at church and to pray more.

"What good will lighting a candle do when I'm sneezing and coughing all the time?" I pleaded.

"It'll do a LOT of good," Camille emphasized.

I gave up and walked away.

"Josie," I was summoned back. I turned around.

"What?" I asked. Gino Jr. was in the living room watching the White Sox game with Uncle Gino and my father.

"We need to talk woman to woman," said Aunt Camille.

I groaned.

Aunt Camille continued, "Women are more susceptible to colds than men."

"I don't need to hear this," I sarcastically moaned.

"It's true, Josie. We are open on the bottom, and men aren't. Be sure you always wear enough underwear to keep warm."

I threw my hands up in the air.

"Enough, please," I said.

"If you don't wear enough underwear," added Carmella, "you'll have continuous colds. I believe that is what troubles you."

"I thought the problem was that I didn't light enough candles," I replied.

Carmella continued, "You're catching drafts by wearing short skirts. You need to cover that area."

I had no idea what they were talking about.

"I wear underwear," I confirmed. "I'm done. This is absurd."

"Enough," said Rose. "Leave her alone." Rose waved her arms around.

My mother interjected, "Let's try what the doctor says."

Camille emphasized, "You don't understand, but someday you'll realize we were right."

My mother took my side, "Let her be. She's an A-student, and the nuns are very fond of her."

Aunt Rose chimed in, "It's good to finally have some brains in this family. It's a welcome change. You going to college, Josie?"

I nodded and told her I was planning to study beyond high school.

"What would you like to be, Josie?" asked Aunt Rose.

I replied that I had no idea but would figure it out once I was in college.

"Go into Journalism," said Dad. "They make good money."

Aunt Rose nodded affirmatively, "That's a good job."

"Maybe," I responded.

"One thing for sure, Josie, is that you don't marry an Italian," Aunt Rose replied. "They got lousy temperaments. Look at your father and your uncle here!"

"Maybe she won't even want to get married." Aunt Camille said.

"Yes, she will," replied Rose. "I just know it."

"I can't say," I noted. "If I meet the right man, I'll probably marry and have children." "I am going to college to study and learn something, not to find a husband."

"Marry a rich guy, Josie," said Aunt Rose.

"The poor ones are a waste of time."

"Well, I haven't even started dating, so who knows? I reminded my aunts.

"Just go slow," reminded Carmella. "You need to meet the right man as there are too many unhappy marriages and miserable kids in this world."

Rose reminded me that if I wanted children I would have to be married or I'd be labeled a 'putana' for the rest of my life. Fortunately, the doorbell rang, and I was rescued as my friend Colleen showed up. She was joining us for dinner.

"How nice!" exclaimed Rose. "Your friend is welcome, Josie!"

Mama was holding a large eggplant. "Look at the nice eggplant Tony brought home."

The family all admired the glossy fruit. My family was very inspired by food.

Colleen approached the room, and I introduced her to everyone. Uncle Gino and my father were glued to the TV set. The White Sox were their #1 priority. Gino Jr. introduced himself.

"Uh, Dad, Uncle Gino, this is my friend, Collen," I shouted.

"Huh?" Neither was interested. "That's a-nice," said Uncle Gino.

My father was oblivious to my voice, and I didn't push it. My aunts were friendly and greeted Colleen.

"You an Irish girl?" Aunt Rose inquired. Colleen nodded.

"That's nice," Aunt Rose smiled.

Gino Jr. commented, "Who cares?"

"You shudda up!" Uncle Gino shouted and cast a threatening look at his son.

Colleen spoke softly, unlike my loud and boisterous family.

"Sit down, everyone!" Mama proclaimed.

Dinner was ready. The food was passed around the table. Everyone was present except the White Sox fans in the living room, which was next to our dining room.

Mama yelled, "I said now! It's ready."

"Shut up," said my father. "I'll put the mal occhio on you!"

"Damn superstitious dago," muttered Aunt Rose.

The Sox finally scored, and my dad yelled, "Look at that son-of-a-bitch run! Woo-Hoo!"

Then the three men joined the ladies at the dining room table. Colleen seemed amused at the family antics. I was sure her family was more sedate.

"Do you know what you're eating, Colleen?" asked my father.

"Uh, yes, it looks like macaroni," she said.

I guess he figured nobody knew what pasta was, other than Italians. I was embarrassed.

My father continued, "I thought you Irish only ate corned beef and cabbage and stew."

Colleen blushed, "Oh, no, sir. We eat spaghetti, hamburgers, and other American stuff, too." "Well, I'll be switched"! dad exclaimed. "Ya' learn somethin' new every day." "Mangia, Colleen."

We all toasted our beverages and ate dinner. Colleen complimented my mother on her food. "Very good, Mrs. Lorenzo." Mom smiled.

I made a general statement that we should change the conversation from cuisine to something else.

"It's no problem," said Colleen. "My family argues sometimes, too."

"This no fight," Uncle Gino said. "A fight is when I talk back to my papa in Italy and he punch-a me in the face."

Uncle Gino was pointing with his fork as it dripped spaghetti sauce all over the tablecloth.

"Don't worry, Gino," said Mom. It'll come out in the wash." Mom appreciated the compliments on her food as she spent most of her day in the kitchen. That was her life. Cooking.

My mother left the table and brought pies and a bowl of fresh fruit, nuts, and nut crackers to the table. Everyone loved her pies; she was a great baker.

Aunt Rose asked, "What are you girls studying now?"

Colleen responded, "Oh, we have algebra, literature, history, and civics. And, of course, religion."

"Gee, things have surely changed!" Rose continued.

"When we went to school, we studied reading, writing, and arithmetic – all in one classroom. I wish I had been born later. I would have enjoyed learning more like you kids. In my time, you went to 8th grade, then you got a job."

"Sounds rough," said Colleen.

"It's rough," said Camille, "We work in a factory because we can't do anything else. Your education is very important."

My father chimed in, "I been tryin' to hit it big at the racetrack for years, but I get nowhere. I got no luck."

"Gambling is no good, Colleen," said Camille. "It gets you nowhere."

Colleen and I loved rock music. We excused ourselves from the table and went into my room. A poster of the Beatles hung above my bed. I put our favorite Beatles records on the turntable and turned the volume up so we could dance. I received a $2.00 weekly allowance and used it to purchase 45rpm records. We danced for a while and then decided we should form a fan club. We decided on a "Wooly Bully" fan club because the Beatles and Rolling Stones already had big fan clubs that we read about in "Sixteen" Magazine. So, we put my 45rpm record of "Wooly Bully" on the turntable and danced the monkey to that hit song by Sam the Sham and the Pharaohs. Colleen and I were going to promote our new fan club at school. We hoped a lot of the girls at school would join and we could all then dance together to my 45rpm records.

My mother called me as it was getting late. Gino Jr. and I walked Colleen home.

"Bye, everybody," said Colleen with a smile.

"Erin go bragh!" yelled Uncle Gino.

A host of adieus bombarded Colleen as we walked out the back door. Colleen lived a few blocks away. It was dark and the streetlights softly glowed. Colleen asked Gino Jr. if he lived nearby.

"No," he said. I live near Lake Michigan, on the northside."

"How nice to be near the beach!" said Colleen.

Gino Jr. nodded. "Is your neighborhood Italian?" Colleen asked.

"No, mostly Jewish," replied Gino Jr. "All of my friends are Jewish."

"What's Jewish?" asked Colleen.

"It's a religion," said Gino. "I don't know much about it, but they go to temples instead of churches."

"What do the temples look like?" Colleen asked.

"They are regular buildings but not as ornate as Catholic churches. The people in our neighborhood are friendly. Even my mom, Rose, is friends with the ladies in the neighborhood. Of course, my mom likes everyone but Father Coco."

Gino then said he was dating a Jewish girl in his class.

"My dad isn't crazy about the idea," Gino said, "but Peggy is nice, and my mom likes her a lot."

We approached Colleen's house, and she thanked us for walking her home.

"See you tomorrow, Colleen."

"See you tomorrow," she replied.

Colleen's mom opened the door, and Gino and I walked home.

Chapter Seven

I couldn't wait to get to school the next day to talk to the girls about the new Wooly Bully fan club. When I woke up, I could smell the coffee. I loved the aroma, and my mom allowed me to have one cup each day once I turned 14. It was my favorite beverage. In fact, after school, I often walked to Delites, a local diner, for a cup of coffee. The server always told me I was too young to drink coffee, but she served me a cup anyway. I ate my cheerios and headed out the door for my walk to school. It was about 6 blocks away from home. As I was walking, my friend, Frank, approached. He was about a half-block away from me.

"Wait up, Josie." Frank attended the public school that was a few blocks away from St. Catherine's.

"What's up, Josie?" he asked.

I told him I was starting a Wooly Bully Fan Club.

"Oh, cool!" he exclaimed. "Who's joining your club?"

So, I explained that I was going to ask the girls at school at lunchtime if they'd like to join, and when the club became famous, it would be listed in "Sixteen" Magazine. I asked Frank if he knew any boys who wanted to join my club.

He responded, "Don't take this the wrong way, Josie, but guys aren't that interested in fan clubs and records."

I guessed that I'd probably wind up with a female club in that case. There was a sock hop coming up in a few weeks, and I asked Frank if he'd like to go with me.

"It's the Daughters of Mary annual dance," I proudly announced.

"Sounds groovy," Frank said that he'd like to go.

"Frank," I said, "It's semi-formal so you need to wear a suit and tie. I will be buying a fancy dress for the dance."

Frank nodded. "I have a suit so it's no problem for me."

When I walked into the door of the school, it was very dark and sterile. A large statue of the Sacred Heart of Jesus loomed over the long hall. The floors were beige tile and green lockers lined the walls. I barely made it to class on time. A loud bell rang as I sat at my desk. Sister Joanna started the prayers. My mind was on the fan club, not the prayer. The morning dragged along, and I couldn't wait for the lunch period. Colleen was standing at my locker, and we walked together to the cafeteria. We ran past the big statue of the Sacred Heart and headed for the basement. I never bought my lunch. My mother always made my lunch for me.

Sister Candida was a short, fat, crotchety, old nun who stood watch as the girls waited in line to buy food. I sat at the customary table with some other pals of mine. We saved a seat for Colleen.

"Young ladies," shouted Sister Candida, "Stop throwing your forks in the garbage can!" or "Will the girl who threw a half-eaten apple in the trash, please see me, or else there will be severe consequences!"

Her comments were always followed by muffled giggles which infuriated her.

"Whoever broke the candy machine, please stand up now!"

More giggles.

My lunch pals were Mary Kay, Marge, Jane, and Mary Pat.

"What's for lunch today, Josie?"

The girls laughed at my lunches which were either pepper and egg or eggplant sandwiches on crusty Italian bread. I loved either one. My friends thought my food was weird, yet I couldn't stand to look at their bologna sandwiches on white bread. Our diets were very different.

When I mentioned the new fan club, the girls didn't seem impressed. Colleen looked shocked. So, as it turned out, Colleen and I were the only members of the Wooly Bully fan club. Jane, a tall, thin, blonde, had never heard of Sam the Sham and the Pharaohs.

Mary Kay said, "Sorry, but I'm dedicated to Herman's Hermits."

Mary Pat said she was already in 3 fan clubs and didn't want to join a fourth. We walked around other tables in the cafeteria to approach other girls, but our efforts were futile. My bright idea went nowhere.

After school, Colleen and I stopped at a local hot dog stand for a Chicago dog and fries. Nobody there was impressed with our fan club either. As it turned out, after Wooly Bully and Little Red Riding Hood, Sam the Sham and the Pharaohs all but vanished. Their singing careers were over.

I walked home after school. Mom could tell something was wrong.

"What's wrong, Josie?" she inquired.

"Nothing, just a crappy day, mom," I responded.

"Josie don't say that word. It's a bad word."

"What?" I asked. "Crappy?"

"Yes," she said. "Use nice words. Don't be a pig like your father."

"Uh, OK, mom," I responded.

"Well, I suppose I should let you know that I have the details on the dance that's coming up. I asked Frankie Torti."

"Oh, that's wonderful." Mom was smiling. "A nice Italian boy."

Mom poured herself a cup of coffee and sat at the kitchen table.

"When did you see Frank?" she asked.

"Oh, this morning, on my way to St. Catherine's."

Mom continued, "Frank is from a nice family. I'm sure you'll have a good time. Go upstairs and talk to Aunt Carmella. I know she'll make a pretty dress for you for the dance. She's an expert at designing, sewing, and tailoring."

I knew Aunt Carmella was a top-notch seamstress. She tried to teach me to sew, but my skills were minimal. At that point, I decided to call Frankie with the details of the dance.

Mrs. Torti answered the phone. "Is this Josie? Oh, hi honey, how are you?"

"I'm fine, Mrs. Torti," I replied.

I knew she liked me because I was Italian. Frankie came to the phone, and I told him the dance was at 8 pm so we could walk down to the school at around 7:30 pm

Frankie asked, "Who else is going?"

I told him that Colleen was bringing Steve, a guy she met at another dance last month.

"Great," replied Frank. "Tell Colleen and Steve to meet us in the coat room at the front of the gym at 7:45 pm.

 "Will do," I replied.

"Great," said Frank. "Bye now."

Now that that was settled, I went to my room and focused on a paper I was writing for my English class. At dinner that evening, I pondered my fan club and decided it was a stupid idea. Mom, Dad, and I sat down to pot roast and vegetables with a salad. Our pet cats were eating their pot roast and vegetables, too.

"How 'ya doing in school, kiddo?" asked my father.

"Good," I replied. "I'm taking Frankie Torti to the school dance."

"Who's he?" he asked.

I told him Frankie was the boy he met one time when I brought him over for dinner. My father looked clueless.

"Oh, yea. That's nice. Pass the bread, Grace."

Dad was more interested in eating at the time. Mom started up.

"Tony, you should be proud of Josie," mom said. "She gets good grades, and her friends are all nice kids. There are a lot of rotten kids nowadays, and we're lucky we don't have one."

Dad responded, "You know those bad kids don't come from no Italian homes, they come from Irish homes with too many kids, and they live like animals!"

"Not true, dad," I said. "My friends all have nice houses."

They did come from big families, though. One of my friends had 11 siblings and a neighbor had 14 children. I know the church didn't allow birth control, but I sure didn't want to have a brood of kids. We finished our dinners.

I said, "Mom, Dad, you know I'm going to Mary Kay's costume party in a few weeks. I need to think of a costume."

Dad said, "Put a stocking on your head and go as a prick! Ha Ha! Ha! Ha!"

Dad loved his little joke, but mom was horrified. "Tony!" she exclaimed. "Watch your filthy mouth!"

"Ah, shad up, Grace. You got no sense of humor!"

I wanted no part of their conversation, so I excused myself from the table. I put my dishes in the sink as dad chuckled at his little joke. My father was a strange person and rather primitive. He was born in 1903 and had a 3rd-grade education. When he was 8 years old, he had to go to work as a peddler to help support his family. Child labor was legal at that time in our history, and my father worked long hours. He could read and write a little. It must have been difficult for him navigating life with such a minimal education.

After dinner, I went upstairs and greeted my two aunts.

"I hope I'm not interrupting anything."

"No, come on in, Josie. I was just putting the dishes away," responded Camille.

Aunt Carmella loved to sew and was at her sewing machine. This was her pastime every night after dinner.

"Aunt Carmella, I'm going to a dance and wonder if you can make a nice dress for me?"

"Oh, sure I can," she said with a smile.

Aunt Camille said, "Excuse me, Josie. I want to wash my hair."

"Sure," I responded.

"Josie, we can work on it together. I'll make the dress and we can do the hem together."

"Great!" I exclaimed.

I asked Aunt Carmella for a short-sleeved dress, A-line, below the knee."

I knew I'd have to get shoes dyed to match the dress. Aunt Carmella approached her dresser and removed a beaded handbag from the bottom drawer.

"You can use my clutch bag, Josie."

"Thanks!" I exclaimed. I was excited to be getting so dressed up for this dance.

"Let's not waste time, Josie. We'll go to the store after work Friday and pick out a pattern for your dress. We can buy the fabric at Marshall Field's."

"WOW!" I exclaimed. "I never bought anything at Marshall Fields. It was such a beautiful store."

Aunt Carmella said, "Fields has good quality merchandise, and you get what you pay for. We'll find something nice."

I was getting more excited by the minute.

Aunt Carmella continued, "We didn't have much growing up so when we started working, your Aunt Camille and I decided to save our money and buy good quality merchandise because it lasts. You save money in the long run. Do you see your Aunt Rose? Always was a slob. Your grandmother used to curse and threaten her, but she refused to pick up after herself and take care of her clothing."

 I told Aunt Carmella that I always picked up after myself because I liked my space to be neat."

Aunt Carmella smiled. "You're like your Aunt Camille and me."

Aunt Carmella continued, "You know our paisanos – the DelVecchios and the DeFrancisco's? They got lots of money, and it shows, but they have no taste. They have ostentatious furnishings in their houses."

I had to admit that my aunt's apartment was tastefully furnished. They liked contemporary furniture and their apartment looked very nice.

"Josie, remember this, Aunt Carmella reminded, "a lot of Italians are showoffs. We grew up with them. You'll see it when you grow up – putting on the dog, bragging, showing off. Italians are famous for it! Our family was never that way. We mind our own business, work hard, and are close to the family. We don't resent anyone's good fortune. We are happy as we are. You have good, strong, peasant blood, Josie. You'll have a happy life. Your father, too, even though he's a louse, works hard. He loads boxes of produce on his truck every day and sells from the truck, putting in long hours. I give him credit for that. Unfortunately, he's a compulsive gambler, or you'd have a nice home, Josie. He's not a good provider."

I asked Aunt Carmella what she thought of my father's sister's home.

"It's beautiful, but everything is covered in plastic, and we have to sit in the basement all the time, so her house doesn't get dirty," I remarked.

"Her house is like a museum, Josie. Who wants to live like that?"

It was time for me to go downstairs. I needed to finish up some homework before bedtime.

Aunt Carmella said, "We'll meet you at Marshall Field's after work on Friday and we can look for fabric for your dress."

"Great!" I was excited.

I rang the doorbell downstairs, and I could hear my parents arguing about who was going to answer the door.

"Answer it!" yelled my dad.

"You get it, Tony. You're right there."

"Aw shit, OK!"   Dad opened the door.

"Use your key next time, dammit, Josie!"

"Sorry, dad," I replied. I ran into my bedroom and slammed the door. I threw my literature book at the door and turned on the record player.

"Help, I need somebody. Help, not just anybody. Help, you know I need someone. Help!"

Chapter Eight

On Friday, I woke up early. I could smell the coffee brewing in the kitchen.

"Mom, I'm meeting the aunts after school tonight. We're going to pick out fabric for my dress for the dance." We're meeting at Marshall Field; they have beautiful fabrics."

Mom had donuts on the table. I grabbed one to eat with my coffee so I could get ready for school. Mom mashed up a plain donut in the cats' food dish. I assumed the poor cats would die from table food, yet they did quite well, all things considered.

"They are my babies," mom said with a smile.

My father complained about the donuts. They were from the Greek store on the corner.

"I don't like that Greek," said dad.

"Anyway, I want 2 eggs and 2 strips of bacon with toast."

Mom prepared dad's breakfast. She had no say-so about anything. She was treated like a servant, and she obeyed his every command. It made me sick, and I decided I'd probably never get married.

When I complained about my father, mom would say, "You have to respect him; he's your father."

I never understand one iota of that. He treated my mother like a slave. I couldn't communicate with her. Their relationship was awful, yet she said she'd never leave him. Were all families like this, I wondered?   I decided I'd move out of the house when I turned 18. Somehow, I'd support myself and go to college. Each year, my resentment of my father and my mother's obedience worsened, and I didn't know how much longer I could stand it.

The school that day was uneventful. After school, I dropped my books off at home and then walked to the corner to catch the bus to the Marshall Field store downtown. The bus ride was always jerky, and I often felt car sick. Between that and the gas fumes, it wasn't pleasant. I couldn't wait to get off. When I arrived at State and Madison Streets, it was a short walk to Field's. I saw the aunts standing in front of the main entrance.

"Let's go to Field's," said Camille, "then we'll have something to eat."

First, we looked at the patterns in the sewing section on the second floor. Then I found a Simplicity pattern that I liked. It was an A-line dress with a scooped neckline and short sleeves. The aunts nodded in approval. Next, we walked over to the fabrics.

"You know brocade is very in," said Carmella.

I was impressed with the brocades and picked out an aqua fabric. Always loved blues and greens. We decided on 2 yards of fabric. When I opened my wallet, Aunt Camille stopped me.

"It's our treat, Josie. We will pay for the fabric."

"Thank you!" I exclaimed.

"You save your money, Josie. You'll need it for college in a few years." I was very thankful.

"We're off to Maling's shoe store now, Josie, so you can find heels that can be dyed to match the dress," Carmella said.

I was excited to no end. I picked out a pair of low heels and gave them to the cashier. She saw the fabric for the dress and clipped a little piece to match the shoes.

"So, Josie, are you ready for dinner?"

"Oh, yes, I'm hungry."

We headed to Lucy's, a favorite delicatessen, on Randolph Street. They made great sandwiches. I was almost 16 and had only eaten at Lucy's a few times with my aunts. I'd never been to a restaurant with my parents. They had no money to dine out, so my poor mom cooked dinner every night.

Aunt Camille said she had a doctor downtown who treated her for allergies.

Aunt Carmella said, "You don't need a doctor. Just light a candle at church and gargle with salt water, and you'll be fine."

"It doesn't work," argued Camille.

"You're a hyperconderac, Camille."

"It's hypochondriac," I reminded.

"That's what I said, Josie," said Carmella.

"And you, Josie," said Camille, "aren't you seeing an allergy doctor?"

"Yes, he's helped me a lot," I said. "I get shots and it's made a big improvement."

"That's because you have faith, Josie. It's more important than the doctor."

I was upset. "Aunt Carmella, those shots have helped me, and I do have faith. The shots are desensitizing me to the pollens I'm allergic to."

Camille shot back, "Leave her alone, Carmella!" "The shots help her, so mind your own bees wax!"

"Hey, please don't argue," I reminded them. "Let's have a nice meal, and then buy some turtle candies at Fannie Mae."

"Yes," said Camille.

Aunt Camille and I both loved turtles -- pecans and caramel covered in chocolate." Best candy ever.

"Josie, please don't forget us someday when we're old. We have no children, you know."

I was stunned. "How could I forget you?"

"Just remember, that's all," said Carmella.

The server approached us and took our orders. Three olive burgers, a coke, and 2 coffees. I asked Aunt Carmella if she'd make my prom dress barely hit my knee.

"Oh, no, Josie! That's not lady-like! Mid-calf is more modest."

"But that's how all the girls wear them," I whined.

"So, you want to be like everyone else?" asked Aunt Camille. "It's always best to be yourself, Josie. Individualism is a treasured trait."

"It's not the style," I argued.

"Good taste is always in style," Aunt Carmella said.

I sadly ate my olive burger.

Aunt Carmella continued, "Josie, you know if you cover up down there, you won't have a runny nose. That will take care of your allergy problem. You tell your allergy doctor about how short you wear your dresses; see if that's causing your problem."

I felt like crying. "Please," I whined again.

"All right, Josie. I'll make your dress the way you want it, but I don't approve," Aunt Carmella said.

I felt a great sense of relief.

We hurried to the bus stop and waited a short time for the bus on Madison Street. I deposited a quarter in the fare box as the bus pulled away from the curb. We sat on a long bench, parallel to the windows. It was warm and stuffy on the bus, so Aunt Carmella turned around and opened a window. A woman in an adjacent seat grunted. Then she grunted again.

Finally, she poked Aunt Carmella in the arm and cackled, "Will you PUH-LEEZ shut that window, Mrs.?"

"No," responded my aunt. "It's stuffy on this bus, and I'm a Miss, not a Mrs."

"No wonder," said the passenger.

"Old Bag!" shouted Aunt Carmella. "Have you looked in the mirror lately?"

Then Aunt Carmella opened the window even more until the passenger moved to another seat. "Ha Ha!" said Aunt Carmella with pride.

Camille beamed, "Your aunt sure has a lot of nerve, doesn't she, Josie?" Carmella was tough and never minced words. Aunt Camille was much quieter.

We exited the bus at our stop and walked to our home. The Brennan kids, all 7 of them, were playing in the street, and old Mr. Leone was giving them dirty looks from his front porch.

"He's nasty," I said to Aunt Camille.

"No matter, Josie. You must respect him as he's an elder. You never know what his life is like."

"Well, that lady on the bus yesterday was your elder. Why did you tell her off, Aunt Carmella?"

"That was different, Josie." We're both adults. A child never talks back to an adult. It's a sign of ill-breeding."

"OK, so anything goes for adults, huh?"

"I didn't say that, Josie. You'll be confronted by different kinds of people when you're an adult, and you still have a lot to learn about interacting with others."

Mom was standing on the front steps.

"Did you finish your shopping?"

"We sure did, Mom," I smiled.

"Thanks, Carm and Cam, it's so nice of you to pay for Josie's dress and shoes."

"She deserves it," said Aunt Camille.

It was late so I decided to finish some homework and then head to bed. I usually listened

to my Japanese transistor radio in bed. Mom thought I was sleeping, but I was listening to

the Top 40 rock and roll hits on WLS Radio.

Chapter Nine

Aunt Mary made my dress so quickly that I couldn't believe it. In a few days, it was completed. I took the bus to Maling's after school, picked up my shoes, and was ready for the dance. Mom loaned me a faux-pearl necklace and earrings. I looked so grown up! Mom took some photographs of me, and I was all set. Frank was due to pick me up any moment. Aunt Camille loaned me a short faux-fur jacket for the evening. She and I were the same size. The doorbell rang, and Frank looked very nice in a dark blue suit, white shirt, and skinny tie. Frank gave me a little box that held a pink and white corsage. I was in heaven.

"Oh, thank you, Frank!" I exclaimed. "Mom, Dad, this is Frank Torti," I said.

"Pleased to meet you." Frank lowered his eyes; he was quite shy.

Dad gave him a quick once-over and said, "Hiya."

"Nice to see you, Frank," beamed my mother.

"Thank you, Mrs."

Mom said, "Frank, what kind of Italian are you?"

It was the old, 'guess the dialect' game.

"Huh?" Frank said.

"Oh, you know, what province in Italy are your people from."

"Oh," he said, my father is Calabrese, and my mother is Naputana."

Frank was serious, but my parents burst into laughter.

"No, no, Frank," mom said. "You mean, "Napoletana. Your pronunciation was a bad word."

Dad roared with laughter. "Naputana, Ha! Ha! He! He! He!"

"Shut up, Tony," mom sternly said. "Don't embarrass Frank."

"What does it mean?" Frank asked.

"It means a lady of the night," said my mother.

"Oh, I didn't mean nothin' by it. Honestly." Frank looked shocked.

"We know, dear. Well, you need to hurry so you're not late for the dance."

My father was still laughing. "Bye," I said, and hurried out the door.

It was cold that evening. Frank held my arm because there were patches of ice on the ground. "Sure is cold, huh, Josie?" Frank asked.

"Yes, it is," I said, not surprised as Chicago has a cold climate.

"Just walk slowly, Josie. It's only a few more blocks to your school."

We stepped from a high curb when I lost my balance.

"Ah, no!!!" I screamed as I fell to my knees in the gutter.

Frank jumped in front of me to stop me from falling on my face.

"My dress!" I cried.

"Don't worry, Josie. It's probably only water."

My dress and shoes were wet, but I couldn't see as it was dark outside."

Frank said, "It'll be OK. I bet nobody will notice."

I hoped that Colleen and Steve were waiting for us in the coatroom, yet I was disturbed that I was wet, although I hadn't seen the worst of it yet.

The gymnasium was on the second floor of my school. Frank and I clomped up the stairs where we heard music playing. At the top of the staircase, Colleen and Steve waited in the coatroom. "Hi," I smiled weakly.

"What school are you from, Steve?" asked Frank.

"If anyone asks, tell them I'm from St. Patrick's, on the other side of the city."

"Why?" asked Frank.

"Because you dummy," said Colleen, "The nuns won't let us bring guys from public schools." "Not a problem, Steve," said Frank.

When I walked into the doorway, Sister John Ellen approached me.

"Josie, what happened?"

Everyone was looking at me. In the bright lights of the gym, horror was visible. My legs were covered in watery mud, and the hem of my dress looked like it had been dipped in filthy water. I burst into tears in front of the entire dance crowd.

"Why me? Why me?   Does God hate me?" I cried out loud.

The dance crowd was laughing as I cried my eyes out. Sister John Ellen tried to calm me.

"Go wash up in the restroom, Josie," she encouraged. "It'll look much better when you rinse most of the mud off."

Frank and Sister John Ellen continued to console me.

"Just wash off your legs, Josie. You'll be OK. I'll go with you, and we'll wash off your nylon stockings," said Sister John Ellen.

"Come on now, you'll be OK," she continued.

"Cheer up, Josie," Frank added.

I walked quickly with Sister John Ellen and headed to the bathroom, glancing downward to avoid the stares in my direction. I was miserable. I removed my stockings, and Sister John Ellen kept trying to cheer me up, saying everything would be fine. She was very compassionate. We rinsed off the nylons and I put the wet stockings back on and waited until I calmed down to go back to the dance.

"Sister," I said, "you don't understand. Everybody's laughing at me. My family hates me. God hates me. Nothing goes right for me."

"Oh, no, Josie," she said. "Don't say that. "Nobody hates you, and God loves you and always will. Many things will happen to you in your life. Some good, some bad; it's all part of life. Our experiences make us who we are," Sister John Ellen said. She was a very kind teacher.

It took me about an hour to calm down. I was angry but composed. I decided that the worst was over.

"Come on, Josie, let's dance."

So, Frank and I danced, but the music wasn't current. The 3-man band must have had an average age of 65, and their music reflected that. What were the nuns thinking? I decided the band must have been cheap because they were so bad. The real highlight of the evening occurred when Steve and Colleen were expelled from the dance because Steve asked one of the nuns to 'grab a priest' and have some fun. Steve thought it was funny, but the nun was horrified.

Chapter Ten

Things were looking up by summer. I had never been on a vacation before, and I was looking forward to going anywhere outside of Chicago. Uncle Gino's cousin, Michael, flew to Chicago for a 2-week visit. Uncle Gino rented a cabin in Wisconsin and invited me to join them. My parents OK'd the trip, and it was just Uncle Gino, Aunt Rose, Michael, and Gino Jr. Michael was a nice fellow. He had a wife and 6 children in Italy. He was very creative – a hairdresser, sculptor, and chef. He did a beautiful job fixing Aunt Rose's very curly hair. He insisted on cooking during his visit, and his eggplant pie was memorable.

We left Chicago on a Friday night. The car was crowded, but we had a nice time telling stories, singing, and sightseeing. I enjoyed the countryside; it was so vastly different from our neighborhood in Chicago. The rented cabin was seated in a heavily wooded area surrounded by tall trees and wild grasses. There was a small lake nearby.

"Thee-sa country is-a very be-oo-ti-ful!" exclaimed Michael. I tell-a my wife all about it."

Gino and Michael ran into the cabin to put on their suits to swim in the lake.

"Come on, Josie," they called.

I just wanted to sunbathe.

"Come on, Josie!"

"Oh, OK." So, I tossed a big beach ball at Gino and jumped in the water.

Uncle Gino didn't bring his guitar because he feared it would fill up with sand.

Meanwhile, Aunt Rose was setting up a nice lunch for us. We sat at a picnic table near the lake and unwrapped sandwiches that Michael had made.

"Delicious, Michael."

We all complimented Michael on the sandwiches.

"Michael, you're a great chef!" Aunt Rose exclaimed.

Uncle Gino saluted Michael. "Delizioso, Michael."

It was just zucchini and egg, but quite yummy.

I started sneezing as it was hay fever season.

"You know, you sneeze a lot, Josie," said Aunt Rose. "Are you nervous?"

"No, why?" I asked. "I have hay fever."

"Well," she said, "you know nervousness causes a lot of ailments. Or it could be because you're away from your mother."

"My mother!" I exclaimed. "She has nothing to do with it. I'm an allergic person. I get weekly shots from an allergist. They are helping, but since I'm outside in the woods, I'm having issues today."

She continued, "When you go to Mass tomorrow, light some candles and see if it helps."

"OK," I sighed, rolling my eyes.

Gino sarcastically said, "Josie, 2 or 3 candles should do the trick."

Uncle Gino reacted, "No, Mr. Smarty-a pants. You make-a fun of the church!"

Uncle Gino was upset. One never was allowed to criticize the church.

Gino and Michael ran back to the water, but I sat at the picnic table with Aunt Rose. A young, blonde-haired man approached us. He looked tired.

"Say, my car broke down on the road about a quarter-mile from here. Might I make a phone call for help? By the way, I'm Jim Wozniak, Father Jim Wozniak." The young man smiled.

"Uncle Gino gasped. "You-a priest? A Cath-o-lic-a priest?"

"Yes, Sir. Are you Catholic?"

"Oh, certainly-a yes! My name is a-Gino Ricci, and this-a woman is-a my wife, Rose."

Aunt Rose smiled, "How do you do, Father." She snubbed her cigarette in the sand.

"I'm Josie Lorenzo, Father, "I said. "Ah-choo!"

"Are you sick, dear?" he asked.

"No, it's just hay fever," I sniffed.

"Oh, it's a miserable malady," he replied, "the bishop has it, too."

"What do you say, Mr. Ricci?" Father Jim asked. "May I use your phone?"

Uncle Gino called to Michael and Gino Jr. They were still in the water.

"Come-a here!" Father Jim-a Something needs help with a stalled car!"

Gino and Michael approached and greeted Father Jim.

Uncle Gino seemed deep in thought.

"How-a do I know he's-a real priest?" he pondered.

"Why would he say he is?" asked Gino Jr.

"Well," Uncle Gino replied, "you know there are a lot of-a nuts out there. You cannot-a be too-a sure. I must give-a him a test!"

"This I gotta see," replied Rose.

"Father, Oh, Father!" Uncle Gino called.

"Since you-a Polish-a priest, I play-a little-a game with-a you."

Father Jim smiled. "What game?"

"I sing-a the Mass and you-a- respond."

Uncle Gino looked suspicious. Father Jim must have thought he was crazy.

So, Uncle Gino chanted, "Dominus Vobiscum."

Father Jim responded, "Et cum spiritu, tuo."

The Gregorian chant continued, "Agnus Dei, Qui tollis pecata mundi…."

"Miserere Nobis," sang Father Jim.

"You pass-a the Cat-o-lic-a test!" Uncle Gino exclaimed, smiling.

Gino Jr. looked embarrassed.

"You wanted to be sure I was a priest, right, Mr. Ricci?"

"How-a you guess?" asked Uncle Gino.

"Just a hunch." Father Jim smiled, and Uncle Gino escorted him into the cabin.

Uncle Gino was ecstatic. "We have-a real holy man-a in the cottage!" he exclaimed.

Aunt Rose shrugged her shoulders.

A tow truck arrived about an hour later. In the meantime, Uncle Gino made cocktails for the adults.

Father Jim said, "I'll have a martini, Mr. Ricci. I haven't had one in years."

If there was anything certain, it was that all priests I ever knew loved a cocktail. Gino Jr. and I drank 7-Up. Uncle Gino then opened his wallet and removed an old photo of a priest.

"This is-a my cousin, Pasquale. He priest in-a my old parish in Palazzo San Gervasia, Potenza, in Ee-taly."

"That's wonderful, Mr. Ricci, but you know, you don't have to talk to clergy about religion all the time. We talk about other things, too," Father Jim said. "Please treat me like you would treat anyone else."

Father Jim seemed like a nice guy.

"You're OK, Father," Aunt Rose remarked, "because you act like a regular person. I've met a lot of priests who thought they were big shots.

"Rose!" Uncle Gino scolded.

"It's OK," said Father Jim, 'Rose can speak her mind."

A knock on the door alerted us to the fact that the tow truck had arrived. Father Jim drank the rest of his martini and headed out the door.

"Thank you all so much for your hospitality," Father Jim smiled.

"Oh, no!" exclaimed Uncle Gino, "I forgot to ask for his blessing."

"Give him a break," said Aunt Rose.

I knew Aunt Rose liked Father Jim. He was nothing like her arch-enemy, Father Coco.

After dinner, I was tired. I grabbed my sleeping bag and pulled it over to a corner of the living room and settled in for the night. I tried to sleep but started wheezing. I jumped up and reached into my purse for another allergy pill. I made the sign of the cross and asked God to please help me. The pill and/or God did the trick, and I was able to fall asleep.

The next morning, Aunt Rose awakened me.

"Josie, have some coffee before we head to church." I gulped down my coffee so I'd have time to shower and dress for church.

"Michael," I asked, "why are you putting the ham in the oven now?"

"Now we can have a nice-a ham dinner after church," he responded.

I offered to drive to church as I had recently received my driver's license. A small Catholic Church was nearby. I was surprised at how small it was compared to Chicago's Catholic Churches which were immense, gothic creations. After Mass, we headed back to the cottage for lunch.

"Mama Mia!" shouted Uncle Gino, "Look at the cow!"

A cow stood by the side of the road. Perhaps he broke through a fence and was lost. When I turned my head to see the cow, I also turned the wheel of Gino Jr.'s red chevy and landed in a shallow ditch.

"What happened," asked Aunt Rose, matter-of-factly.

"Oh, Jesu!" exclaimed Michael.

Gino Jr. said, "It's your fault, Pop, for distracting Josie with the cow."

"You're a real prize, Gino," said Aunt Rose dryly. I started to cry.

"Let's stand outside and try to flag down some help." In a short while, a woody station wagon pulled over behind us.

An older man said, "I see you need some help." He smiled.

"I have a rope we'll connect to your bumper, and we'll get you out in a jiffy."

Uncle Gino smiled, "You nice-a man! Grazie. You E-Italiano?"

The man smiled, "Oh, no! I'm as American as apple pie. Come from a long line of German farmers who settled here many years ago."

The kind man tied our car to his and gently pulled us out of the ditch. I profusely thanked him. He smiled again and wished us a nice Sunday. Uncle Gino offered the man a 5-dollar bill. "Buy you-a self a nice bottle of wine."

The kind man refused, "Oh, no need, sir. It was my pleasure, a good deed for the day."

And our kind stranger drove off.

"What a nice man," said Aunt Rose, blowing cigarette smoke in the kind man's direction.

"I'll drive but I promise I won't be distracted," I commented.

We rode back to the cottage, everyone in a good mood. When Uncle Gino opened the front door, smoke poured out.

"Managgia!" he exclaimed. "There's a fire in the oven!"

Michael ran into the house and started opening the windows.

"My ham, Madonna!"

I placed a handkerchief over my mouth and helped open windows. Gino Jr. opened the back door in the kitchen, and Michael stabbed the flaming ham with a large meat fork and flung it out the back door. It landed in the grass. We all ran outside and let the house air out. Michael took the hose and extinguished the burning ham. It was a black blob on top of the green grass, an interesting sight. We all sat in the backyard at a picnic table as the house aired out. That stove needed a good cleaning, and Aunt Rose thought that the ham ignited for that reason.

"I'm starving," said Gino Jr.

Michael blurted out, "I got an idea!" He ran into the kitchen and returned with a meat cleaver, a loaf of bread, and a platter.

"Now we gonna eat!" he exclaimed.

As he cut off the outside burnt layer, the inside of the ham revealed a lovely pink interior.

"It joost-a burns on-a the outside. Now we eat."

That afternoon we enjoyed delicious, juicy ham sandwiches. We laughed at how what

seemed to be a ruined day, turned out to be a pleasant afternoon in the backyard.

Chapter Eleven

During the 1970s a few things changed. Gino Jr. fell in love with a Jewish girl who he wished to marry. The family was in an uproar. As it turned out, Peggy said she couldn't marry a gentile, and that romance went nowhere. Then, a few years later, she married a Catholic pre-med student at Northwestern University. Gino Jr. was heartbroken.

My college life was interrupted. I fell in love with a nice boy named Ted Sliwa. We both dropped out of school, married, and started attending night classes to complete our degrees. Dad was angry that I didn't marry an Italian, but he got over it pretty quickly and did like Ted. He didn't like the fact that Ted was tall, and my family looked like midgets next to him, but I didn't care about height. It seemed to bother my father though.

He said, "You know, you might have a 6-foot-tall daughter!"

I said, "So what? She can play basketball."

Dad had some issues with height. My mother liked Ted, so I ignored my father's height concerns.

The first time Ted met my family, we all gathered around the dining room table, and everyone introduced themselves to my fiancé.

Aunt Rose smiled, "I'm Rose, Josie's aunt."

Camille and Carmella introduced themselves, too, and seemed very pleased to meet Ted.

"Hi, Ted." My dad handed Ted a beer.

One thing my father greatly approved of was Ted's love of the White Sox. My father, too, was a White Sox fan. It was about all they shared in common.

"Hey, paisano, let's watch-a the ball game after dinner," Uncle Gino smiled.

I knew Ted liked that idea.

Aunt Rose suddenly looked very sad.

"Did you know that a 14-year-old girl was raped right down the street from us?"

"Filthy animals!" shouted Aunt Camille.

"The newspaper reports such terrible things," said Aunt Carmella.

"You know, Josie," commented Uncle Gino, "there's no rape-a in-a E-taly."

"Of course, there is," I said. "It's universal." Aunt Rose continued. "It's because men are animals and can't control themselves. In Europe, they tend sheep. They leave the women alone." "What?" I nearly jumped out of my seat. "Are you condoning animal abuse?"

"Better a sheep than a young girl," replied Rose.

"I give up," I said. Then Rose added, "If the woman gets pregnant, does she have a sheep or a baby?"

"You're all crazy! A woman can't have a sheeple or anything else. You can't hybridize species!"

"Josie, I asked an honest question," said Aunt Rose. "Calm down," said Rose, "I guess it makes sense. I never heard a baby utter baa-baa."

 Everyone started laughing. Ted must have thought they were all nuts.

Then my father chimed up with this story.

"You'll get a kick out of this!"

Then he told the family that the bathtub wouldn't drain, so he called a plumber. The plumber pulled the plug from the drain to release the water. Aunt Rose burst into laughter.

"Tony, don't tell that story. You sound like a real dope."

"Wait for a second," argued my father. "That bastard charged me for a house call. He should-a did it for free."

"Dad," I said, "Nothing is free." For once in his life, he agreed with me.

"You know," he continued "I may stop peddling. I'm getting tired."

"How old are you?" asked Ted.

"I am 69."

Ted was surprised because my father looked like he was in his 50s.

"You look great!" said Ted.

"That's because peddling ain't easy," dad replied, "you do a lot of lifting of heavy crates of produce and you work long hours, staging, selling, and weighing the goods."

"How old are you, Ted," asked my father.

"I'm 26."

"Oh, you're too young, wasting the best years of your life getting married."

I was angry that my father said that to Ted.

"I have a surprise," said my mother.

"What?" Rose inquired.

"I start a full-time job tomorrow."

Everyone was surprised. My mother had not worked in over 20 years. She felt she needed to be home to take care of my father and me.

My mother beamed, "I'm going to be a general clerk at Amalgamated Van Lines. I can even walk to work and walk home for lunch."

My father laughed, "Yes, you work, and I'll make pasta fagioli for dinner for you when you come home."

Sadly, that didn't happen. My mother did it all, worked, cooked, and cleaned the house. My father did nothing around the house, even though he was now retired.

My mother continued, "Since Tony retired, our income is very low. My salary will help us to get by."

I asked my mother what she did before I was born; she said she was a file clerk at Sears. Sears, Roebuck & Company was headquartered on the west side of Chicago, and they employed many of the residents at that time.

Uncle Gino chimed in with, "You know, Ted, you marry into a very important Italian family?" Uncle Gino seemed so serious, which was out of character for him. He was usually good-natured and loved to tell jokes.

Ted seemed surprised. "I didn't know you were an important family," he replied.

"Oh," continued Uncle Gino, "I enlisted in the E-talian-a army in World-a War One. I was-a sixteen, and I got-a promoted to Corporal. I important in-a big war."

I responded, "Uncle Gino, I didn't think Italy was that important in World War One. Weren't they on the wrong side?"

"Joosta min-oot, Josie," Uncle Gino went on. "No country want to fight-a Italy because we was-a so good. We so good that no E-talian died."

"Oh, brother!" I exclaimed.

I could see Ted was ready to start laughing.

He commended Uncle Gino and said, "I'm happy to know a man who served in World War One."

Uncle Gino responded, "You smart-a-boy, even if you-a Polish boy. I'm glad-a Josie marry a boy with a short-a hair, no hippie-a bums!"

"What does it matter how a person wears their hair?" I asked.

"Oh," said Aunt Rose, "it matters a lot."

The aunts nodded in agreement.

"You see those-a long-hair bums, they a bunch-a Comm-oo-nistas!"

Rose grabbed Uncle Gino's arm. "Calm down. Italy had Mussolini in the second war, and he was a no-good Fascist!"

Uncle Gino was outraged. "Mussolini was a kill-a by the E-talian people. We no want-a Fascista!"

"Keep your trap shut," said Rose, "and change the subject. God help me!" moaned Rose. Uncle Gino added, "You know they got-a no hippie in E-taly. The government no allow it."

I tried to tell Uncle Gino that there were hippies everywhere, but he didn't believe me. (A few years later, Uncle Gino and Aunt Rose flew to Italy to see Uncle Gino's sister, Franca. When they landed in Rome, a large gathering of hippies was protesting something at the airport. Uncle Gino was horrified and said he'd never return to Italy after this trip.)

After dinner, Aunt Rose asked if we'd found an apartment yet.

"We have to check out a few places," I replied.

"Where are you looking?"

I said, "Woodlake."

A chorus of family members seemed puzzled. "Woodlake?"

My father said, "I know a lot of your people live there, Ted."

"What are you talking about?" I asked, completely irritated.

"I mean a lot of Polish live in Woodlake," he said.

"It's all right to live among your own," said Aunt Rose.

"We are not moving there because it's a Polish neighborhood," I firmly stated.

"We are moving there because rents are cheap, it's near the El, and we can get downtown and to our night classes easily from that location." We can't afford Chicago. One-bedroom apartments are $200 per month."

"My God!" shouted Carmella.

"We can get a one-bedroom in Woodlake for $135. We plan to live there until we can afford to save up a down payment for a house."

"Buy a house, it's a good investment," replied Uncle Gino. "Until then, you live-a with your people, Ted."

"Stop that," I replied. We're moving there because it's cheaper than Chicago and has good transportation. We don't care who lives in that neighborhood. Case closed."

I was embarrassed that Ted had to see the continual goofiness of my relatives.

Dad asked Ted if he played the horses. He frowned when Ted said he preferred football and baseball to horse racing.

"Josie," asked Aunt Camille, "would you like to come for dinner next Friday?"

"Sure, Aunt Camille. Ted and I are free."

After the group went home, my parents, the pets, and I all retired for the evening.

Chapter Twelve

Mom started her new job on Monday. I was very happy for her, and she was thrilled to start a new line of work. Dad promised to prepare his first dinner for the family. When my mother arrived home after her first day at the new job, I couldn't wait to hear about it. The first thing she did when she entered the house was pet the cats as they rubbed up against her legs.

"Mom, how was your new job?"

"Oh, marvelous! I work with two other girls my age and they are friendly. I'm tired, but it's worth it."

I felt my mother had a real social life outside of the family with her new job, and I was happy for her.

"I was introduced to the others in the office, and it's a lot to remember, but everyone seemed nice. I had lunch in the cafeteria with Louise and Mary, but I don't think they are Italian."

"Who cares, mom, as long as they are nice people," I said.

Mom continued, "We all brought our lunch and I ate a cheese Danish at coffee break. Not low calorie, but it was really good."

Mom was smiling, and it was nice to see her beautiful smile. I think the job opened a new world for her.

Mom then said, "My boss is Mr. Vance. He's a colored man and very nice."

Dad quickly turned from the oven, "You mean melanzani?"

My father called Black people melanzani which is an eggplant in Italian. Not nice, but this family was not enlightened.

"I'll be switched," said dad.

"Oh, I like my boss," continued mom, "He's very nice and well-to-do. He lives in Oakbrook." "Geez, he must be loaded!" exclaimed my father.

"He must make good money, and he doesn't even do any heavy lifting," said my mother.

I tried to explain that not all jobs require heavy manual labor, and Mr. Vance might have other types of pressure to perform his job.

"What pressure?" intoned dad. "He doesn't lift cases of melons and sacks of potatoes all day. That's pressure on your back!"

Mom then smiled and said, "There's a big party on Saturday night at the Sheraton to commemorate the company's 25th anniversary. Your father and I are going."

"I ain't goin'," said dad.

"What do you mean, Tony?" asked mom, noticeably irritated. "It's free."

"Oh, OK. If it's free, I'll go. Dinner's ready; sit down."

So, I sat down at the table as my father served a black meatloaf. It looked like a brick. Large chunks of onions protruded from it. At least the salad looked edible.

"Josie," dad said, "this is gonna be the best meal of your life." I seriously doubted it but smiled weakly.

"I betcha dollars to donuts, it's better than your mother's meatloaf."

Mom was insulted, as she was a good cook and spent a good deal of time preparing meals for us. Dad took a serrated knife and started sawing slices of the black meatloaf.

"Why is it so hard?" I asked.

The meatloaf took a bit of sawing, but I managed to put a tiny piece in my mouth. "UGH!" I yelled. "This is inedible!"

"What the hell's wrong with you?   This is a great meatloaf."

Dad put a big crunchy piece in his mouth. "Ummm, dee-licious!" he exclaimed.

Mom took a bite and wrinkled up her nose. "Tony, it's awful. What's in it?"

Dad proudly recited his recipe: "One pound of beef, two big onions, and eight cloves of garlic."

"No wonder my stomach is on fire!" I said with watery eyes.

"Tony, you need breadcrumbs and an egg, and no garlic is necessary," mom instructed.

"It might be dry," said dad, "but your meatloaf is juicy and has no flavor."

"Tony," mom implored, "please use the cookbook next time."

I tried to console my father. "Don't be offended, dad. We know you tried."

My goal was to accommodate his large Sicilian ego.

"Eat the salad, then," he yelled. "I'll eat the meatloaf." The salad was edible, and I complimented my father on his salad. He pouted and didn't say much, just cold stares across the table.

"Gotta go," I said. "Picking up Ted tonight to go apartment hunting."

"And why is that?" dad asked.

"His car is in the shop, and I don't mind driving."

"Well, girls shouldn't be driving men around. Don't make this a habit."

My father was mentally living in another century. Ted and I wound up renting a 4 room apartment in an old yellow brick building. It was old but clean and affordable. Only $135 per month; while most of the apartments we previously viewed were close to $200 per month, that was unaffordable for us. So, Ted and I rented the apartment on the spot. We gave the property owner, Mr. Schmirler, a deposit and found our new apartment. It was near the El and an easy ride to downtown Chicago, work, and our night classes at the university. The property owner made us promise that we wouldn't live there until we were married, and we gave him our promise. When we told Mr. Schmirler that we both lived with our parents, he seemed very pleased.

"That's what I like," he confirmed, "kids who live at home until they marry."

Then the property owner said that his two daughters still lived at home also. We told the property owner we'd be having furniture delivered, and he didn't object to that. Ted then asked me if I was nervous.

"Sure," I said, "but it feels right to me."

Ted beamed. "Do you think your folks like me?" he asked.

"Well, this is silly," I replied, "Dad thinks you are too tall but, otherwise, I feel he does like you, but just won't admit it. He's stubborn as a mule."

We drove back to my house to tell my parents the good news. When I opened the front door, my parents and Aunt Camille were yelling.

"You don't trust your daughter," cried mom.

"Go back to the gutter where you belong, you Sicilian scum!" yelled Aunt Camille.

Then I heard dad scream. "I bet she's screwin' that Pole."

Ted's eyes almost popped out of his head. My face was on fire and, I yelled as loud as I could. "I heard that, you ignoramus!"

"Josie!" mom exclaimed in horror.

My father raised his fist. Mom and Aunt Camille gasped.

"No, Tony!" mom screamed.

"Shut your mouth," I said, "or I'll have Ted knock your lights out!"

Dad lowered his fist.

My mother was in tears. "Have some respect, Josie. He's your father."

"Respect! Respect!" I screamed. "Why is there no respect for me?"

I stalked out the door and dragged Ted behind me. He was horrified. I don't think he was accustomed to our loud, nasty fights.

"I'm not going back there," I cried to Ted. "I'm sick of the whole lousy, narrow-minded, ignorant bunch who demand respect and don't listen!"

"Calm down, Josie," Ted reassured me. We'll be married in less than two months, and we have a nice apartment; everything will be fine.

"I don't want them sticking their noses in our business and insulting me."

"It will all be OK; you'll see."

Chapter Thirteen

Things cooled off at home and Ted and I were looking forward to dinner with the aunts. We also wanted to tell them all about our apartment. Camille answered the door, grinning from ear to ear.

"Come on in! I made a surprise dinner."

We hurried up the stairs and Carmella greeted us. We were welcomed with hugs and kisses.

The smell of fresh flowers drew my attention to the living room. Atop the television sat a photo of my late grandmother, surrounded by red and white carnations. A votive candle burned in front of the photo. To the left was a statue of St. Anthony, laying on its side. Behind this funereal assortment loomed a large crucifix.

"What is that?" asked Ted.

"It's a shrine," said Carmella. "We pray that St. Anthony and Grandma will help your allergies go away."

"Are your allergies better?" asked Camille.

"Yes," I said, "due to the medication I'm taking."

I was corrected, "No, Josie. It's Grandma and Saint Anthony who are helping you."

Next, I heard Camille declare that dinner was ready. The dinner smelled good.

"I made this for you, Ted," said Aunt Camille. "Roast pork and sauerkraut and bread dumplings."

Aunt Camille had found the recipes in a cookbook at the local library.

"That was nice of you, Aunt Camille," I said.

"Smells wonderful!" exclaimed Ted.

He was escorted to the head of the table.

"The man always sits at the head of the table," reminded Aunt Carmella.

I felt like I was living in the dark ages. Once the seating order was established in a family, it was never broken.

"Now, Josie, tell us all about your apartment."

I explained that the apartment was 4 rooms in an old building, clean, and very affordable.

"Is the bathroom near the bedroom?" Camille inquired, as she placed a large platter of roast pork on the table.

"Don't interrupt, Camille," scolded Carmella.

"Shut up, and stop telling me what to say and do," argued Camille.

"Ouch! That's hot!" Carmella jumped from the table when she touched a bowl of gravy that was steaming.

She ran into the kitchen to run her hands under cold water.

"That's what you get!" said Camille. "Keep quiet and let Josie finish."

"Are you OK, Aunt Carmella?" I asked.

"Yes, all's well."

Camille passed a large bowl of salad around the table.

"Where did I leave off?" I asked.

"I asked if the bathroom is near the bedroom."

"Pass the applesauce," said Camille.

Carmella barked, "Shut up and let Josie talk!"

"Why do you ask about the bathroom?" I asked.

Carmella's response was, "When you're newly married, make sure your bathroom is near the bedroom for personal reasons. You'll understand after you are married awhile."

I was befuddled.

"Does this have to do with sex?" I asked.

"Shh! Josie! Don't bring that up in mixed company!" scolded Carmella.

"No more. No more!" said Camille.

"Fine," I said. "No more questions, please."

To this day, I still don't know what she was talking about."

I explained that we ordered furniture for our apartment.

"Delicious meal, Aunt Camille."

"Yes," Ted heartily agreed with me.

"It's heavy food, isn't it?" asked Camille. "Italian food is much lighter," she replied.

"What do you mean," I asked.

"Well, pasta and vegetables are so soft that you can just mush them up and swallow them with no chewing, no effort."

I didn't care to engage in another ridiculous conversation and nodded in agreement.

We cleared the dishes from the table and then Camille brought out a luscious poppy seed cake for dessert. Ted was thrilled as it was one of his favorites.

"You're a great cook, Camille," complimented Ted.

Aunt Camille blushed and thanked him. Carmella told Ted that Camille was always in the kitchen cooking. It was true, and she was a terrific cook.

"I like to make a nice meal," said Camille. "Carmella here couldn't fry an egg if she was starving."

Carmella objected. "You cook as a hobby because you like to cook, just as I sew because I enjoy sewing."

A fight ensued over whether cooking and sewing were hobbies or work. Ted and I just shut up and stared blankly at each other.

"You pour over cookbooks!"

"You spend too much time looking over patterns!"

"Hey, come on, don't fight!" I implored.

This bickering was so commonplace in my family that it became the unwelcome norm. Nonetheless, I was exhausted by it.

"Change the subject, will you?" I asked.

Camille and Carmella exchanged dirty looks as I described the furniture we ordered.

"Our furniture," I continued, "is contemporary."

"That's nice," the aunts agreed.

Camille opened with, "You know Minnie Roberto on our mother's side?"

"No," I said. I just knew this would end up in another insane conversation.

"Sure you do, Josie! She was at Vito Chiaramonte's funeral."

"No, I don't," I confirmed.

"Oh, sure you do," said Carmella. "She's Angelo DiPrima's wife's brother's second cousin on his mother's side."

"Who's Angelo DiPrima?" I asked.

"Oh, come on now, Josie. You know Angelo DiPrima!" smiled Carmella.

"Where is this conversation going?" I asked.

"Something or other about furniture," Ted commented.

"Ah, yes," smiled Camille. "Well, Minnie Roberto's daughter invited us over for coffee last Wednesday, and she had all Spanish-style furniture. It was nice." Camille smiled. "The only thing I didn't like was that wrought iron thing with candles hanging in her foyer. It was gaudy." Carmella agreed. "I didn't like it either."

"Josie wouldn't buy one of those things. She has good taste," said Camille.

"I think that's a sconce, Aunt Camille." I advised the aunts that our décor would be much simpler." Ted pushed himself from the table.

"That was a memorable dinner," said Ted.

I confirmed that dinner was wonderful.

Then Carmella pulled a box out of the pocket of her housedress.

"It's a little present for you, Josie."

"Thank you," I said.

I opened the box to find a pin cushion that looked like the earth. I wondered where my aunts found it.

"Thank you both," I said. "It's very nice."

I didn't think Ted knew what it was. The aunts beamed, and I was happy they were pleased. They were from a different era but were very loving. I offered to help with the dishes, but the aunts refused.

"You are our guests, kids. Have a seat in the living room."

Ted and I moved to the living room and sat on the sofa. Dishes, pots, and pans clanged in the kitchen. The aunts walked into the living room to join us. They put a recording of "La Traviata" on the turntable, and Ted and I tolerated the opera as we knew it made them happy. To this day, I can't listen to opera. I believe I overdosed on it throughout my younger years.

Chapter Fourteen

Mom's employer, Amalgamated Van Lines, was celebrating its 25th anniversary. Aunt Carmella made a blue A-line dress for her to wear to the company dinner. Mom bought 2 additional tickets so Ted and I could join her and dad at the dinner. We weren't thrilled about attending but decided to go to the dinner with my parents to make Mom happy. Dad was not thrilled.

"Jeeeee-sus! I hate goin' to this thing."

"Never mind," scolded Mom. "I am new to this job, and the least you can do is attend the dinner with me. Ted and Josie are joining us, too."

Dad groaned, "But Lollipop Lu is running in the 4th race, and I got a good feelin' about that horse!"

Dad stuffed his arms into an old suit that reeked of mothballs.

"Who gave you the tip on that horse?" asked Mom.

"One of my old friends," dad pouted.

"Your old friends are all in the cemetery. That's a load of bull!"

"Never mind!" shouted dad. "I got me some friends who gave me a tip on that horse."

"Who?" asked Mom.

"My brother, Frankie."

"Frankie!" said Mom. "You haven't spoken to him in almost 30 years!"

"Well," explained my father, "I took a ride last week past Frankie's house. His fat wife, Theresa, answered the door. Frankie jumped up and gave me a big hug like nuthin' ever happened." It was nice to talk again.

"Your brother is a crook!" exclaimed mom. "Why do you even want to talk to that guy?

He tried to cheat you on a business deal 30 years ago and you stopped talking. It was a blessing not to talk to that swine ever again!"

"So, I am glad we're talkin' again," said Dad.

"I guess so," said Mom. "Family is blood, and you must always stick together."

I didn't understand my mother.

"Mom," I asked, "why associate with someone who is a crook?" She replied, "It's your blood. You must always stand up for your own blood."

I sighed. "Come on, Ted. Let's go."

The drive to the Sheraton ballroom was short. We checked our coats and walked into the lovely ballroom.

Mom was in awe. "I never saw anything this beautiful since Antoinette Escarola's wedding in '56."

"Who's that, mom?" "Oh, Josie," she smiled.

"You know Antoinette. She's Francie Chiaramonte's former husband's godfather's daughter-in-law! Now you remember?"

I didn't, but said, "Sure, mom." It was self-preservation. I had to say I remembered Antoinette; otherwise, I'd hear the entire history of Antoinette Escarola and Francie Chiaramonte.

Mom continued, "She married Bruno Rigati, Vito Cantalupo's cousin."

"I remember, mom. Really," I fibbed.

"Hey, they got an open bar here," said Dad. Then he, Mom, and Ted went to pick up drinks at the bar. Ted ordered a scotch and water. I went to our table. Ted knew I would only drink a screwdriver, so he ordered one for me. Mom didn't drink alcohol, so she ordered a 7-Up.

Ted said, "Why not order an alcoholic drink?"

Mom responded, "No, I'll stick with 7-Up."

Dad, surprisingly, ordered a martini. He normally drank beer, so we were all surprised.

"Dad, why the martini? You never order anything but beer," I inquired.

"I just want to try one," he replied.

Mom pointed to a handsome African-American man at our table.

"That's my boss; he's very nice to work for," she said.

"So," said Dad, "you work for a...."

"Stop it, Tony!" Mom scolded, "He's a very good man!"

Dad shrugged.

"Mom, try my screwdriver." She did but puckered her lips.

"Too strong. It would be better without the alcohol."

My father picked up his martini glass. "Look at this!" he exclaimed. "No damn olive! They got lousy help today. When I was young…."

"Please, Dad! Let's not hear about the martinis in the Jazz Age."

Mom changed the subject, "Let's go meet my boss, Mr. Vance."

"Why?" scowled Dad.

We walked over to Mr. Vance, and I sincerely hoped Dad would keep his mouth shut and smile. Mr. Vance and his wife were beautifully dressed. They certainly had good taste. He stood when he saw my mom approaching the table.

"Ah, Grace! So nice to see you!"

Mom blushed. "Thank you, Mr. Vance. I'd like you to meet my family."

"Sit please," he said as he motioned to the chairs.

When we sat down, my father smiled nervously and quickly shook Mr. Vance's hand, almost as though he was afraid to touch him. Ted and I greeted the Vance's. They were very personable and easy to talk to. Too soon, Dad finished his martini which concerned me.

"Hey, let's get more drinks!" Dad exclaimed.

Dad took drink orders and returned with a tray filled with drinks, including his second martini. I was worried. He had a goofy smile on his face.

"Hey, Grace," he said, "What's that joke you know about martinis, martoonies. Ha! Ha! It was a damn good joke!"

"I don't remember it," mom said. I knew she was worried.

"Come on, baby! Tell that joke!" My father was drunk.

The volume of his voice increased to an uncomfortable level.

 "Come on, Grace. Tell the joke! Hee! Hee! Ha! Ha!"

Mr. Vance wisely changed the conversation. "What line of work are you in, Tony?"

"Oh, I'm in produce, all my life. But now I'm too old to load crates of bananas, cantaloupes, eggplants, sacks of potatoes, you know."

Mom interrupted. "Enough, Tony. Mr. Vance understands."

"He's retired now," she added.

My father downed his second martini.

"You wanna' see somethin', Mr. Vance? I bet you can't do this!"

Dad stuck his tongue out, wiggled it like a snake, and touched the tip of his nose with it.

"Tony!" Mom yelled. "Stop it! We're at a dinner, not at some tavern!"

She was very upset, and I felt bad for her. Ted looked troubled, too.

"The food is coming out already." I said, "and the salad looks very good."

Dad stood up. "I think I'm gonna get me one more martini," he mumbled.

He stumbled and mom gave him a swift kick in his leg.

"Ouch! What the F…" He grimaced, as my mother must have given him quite a kick.

"No more drinks!" she demanded.

"OK," he groaned.

The dialogue was sparse during dinner. The Vance's were surely shocked at my father's behavior. The food was good, and we all hoped my father would sober up after eating his dinner. At that time, the president of Amalgamated Van Lines entered the stage.

"Good evening, employees and friends of our company. It's a real pleasure to address you this evening, on our Twenty-fifth Anniversary."

My father drooled. "I bet that son-of-a-bitch has money to burn, Eh?"

Mom gave him another swift kick under the table.

"Dad, be quiet," I quietly demanded.

Mr. and Mrs. Vance listened to the speaker and ignored my father. I was embarrassed to be related to him. Ted looked at me with sympathy. Mom was miserable.

My father lit up a cigar. "I bet that guy's a Republican. They are a bunch of rich assholes."

Another kick from mom.

"Ouch!" he exclaimed.

People at the next table looked at us in horror.

"Goddam Republicans…," he muttered.

I glared at him and hoped he got the message to keep his mouth shut. For most of the rest of the evening, he quietly puffed on his smelly cigar and, thankfully, kept quiet. As the lights dimmed and the dance music started, Mr. and Mrs. Vance quietly waltzed away. I was glad they had escaped the embarrassment of our table. Ted and I arose to dance, leaving my parents to duke it out. To my surprise, my parents stood up and started to dance. Mom danced as dad stumbled on the dance floor.

My father then pulled a handkerchief from his pocket and started waving it wildly in the air. "Hey! Hey! Tarantella! Let's play some lively music!"

He spun around, waving his hankie. My mother burst into tears and ran out the door. Ted and I grabbed him and dragged him away.

"Hey, I'm havin' me a good time!"

"You ruined Mom's evening!" I shouted.

I viewed him with pure disgust. Ted ran up to my mother and hugged her.

"I'll be a laughingstock at work," she sobbed.

"No, you won't, mom," I consoled her.

"People will just wonder what's wrong with your husband. They'll feel sorry for you. I sure do."

Chapter 15

I was now married for a year. The family was coming for dinner, of course. Ted planned to barbecue chicken.

I answered the phone. "Hello?"

It was Aunt Camille. "I just wanted to see how last-minute preparation is going," she said. "Oh, fine," I replied.

"I just wanted to check on the menu," Aunt Camille said.

"Why?" I asked.

"What are you cooking?" she questioned.

"We're having a barbecue," I responded. "You know, chicken, potato salad, and sliced tomatoes from our garden."

"Did you at least make mostaccioli?" she asked.

"Well, no. I didn't think it fit in with an all-American style dinner."

Aunt Camille sighed. "Josie, mostaccioli ALWAYS fits in with any meal. Besides, you know our family always has pasta with our Sunday meal." She sounded exasperated.

"But I made potato salad, Aunt Camille, that's two starches," I reasoned.

"Never mind. I'll bring some over," she insisted.

"I'm also bringing tortoni that I made."

"But I made an apple pie for dessert," I insisted.

"Remember? I said all-American dinner?"

I was frustrated that I couldn't even plan my meal.

"Not another word, Josie. We're all set for dinner."

This time, I sighed. "OK. I need to go, Aunt Camille. I have quite a bit left to do. Bye!"

Ted entered the room. "What's wrong?"

"I don't know why I can't serve what I want for our barbecue, Ted," I moaned.

"It's the old-timers," he said. They still like to do things their traditional way, and they always bring food to someone's home. It's their culture."

Next, my mother called to tell me she was bringing a pizza.

"Fine." I didn't say much else. It was futile to try to reason with this family.

"Listen," my mother said. "Don't say anything about your father's new part-time job."

"What job?" I asked.

"Well, he got a part-time job as a janitor, but they fired him after a day for foul language." "OK, mom. I got it. I know he can't work for other people. He's primitive. I already warned Rose, Camille, and Carmella to not mention Tony's part-time job."

Mom continued, "Did you receive Sears' summer catalog?"

"Yes, I replied."

"OK," she said. "I received two, so I'll bring you one."

"Mom, I already have it."

"That's OK, I'll bring it anyway," she responded.

"Fine. See you soon," I replied.

I felt I had a real communication problem with my family. It seemed they never listened to a thing I said. Or was it me? Was I doing something wrong?

The doorbell rang.

When Ted opened the door, Uncle Gino yelled, "Happy Anniversary! Where's-a the bride?" "Come on in," said Ted.

I ran to the front door to greet Aunt Rose, Uncle Gino, and my cousin, Gino. Gino was still a bachelor but had a good job and a nice condo on the lakefront.

"Happy, Happy!" said Aunt Rose, handing me a jug of red wine and a jar of olives.

"They're for my martini," she reminded.

Ted scurried around, preparing drinks for the group, as the aunts and my parents arrived shortly after. We all sat in the living room when Uncle Gino announced that he was going to tell a dirty joke.

"Oh, you're going to hear it sooner or later," said Aunt Rose. "Your uncle likes to tell this joke, and he feels now you're old enough to hear it. Personally, I'm sick of it. Go ahead, Gino."

Rose lit her cigarette and leaned back in her chair.

Uncle Gino began, "A man, he goes-a into the hardware-a store and he says, "I wanna' buy a doorknob. A young-a sales lady hands it to-a him and-a say, 'Here it is, you need a screw?' And the man-a he says, 'No-a thank you. I pay cash!'"

Uncle Gino burst into laughter. Everyone smiled. I knew they'd heard this joke before. Ted and I chuckled.

"I need to start the grill," Ted announced.

Aunt Rose asked me if I needed help. I thanked her and said everything was done. I'd made potato salad, coleslaw, and baked beans, and the table was set.

Aunt Rose smiled. "You kids today are so smart. You plan everything in advance, the menu, table setting, everything. I love this generation."

"How nice, Aunt Rose," I said.

"No, she's-a wrong," insisted Uncle Gino. "Keeds-a today are a bunch-a-bums. I give you and-a you cousin, Gino, a test. What was the sermon about at church this morning?"

Uncle Gino knew that Gino Jr., Ted, and I didn't attend Mass any longer. There was no response.

"See?" Uncle Gino said, "I told you…all a bunch-a bums. You kids no go to the church! Today, the priest-a talk about the loaves and-a fish."

Gino Junior sighed.

"You watch it-a buster," Uncle Gino said, as he shook his fist in his son's direction.

Then he scolded Gino for not yet being married and asked me why I wasn't pregnant after a year of marriage.

"You Polish-a husband kind of slow?" he asked.

Cousin Gino and I said nothing.

Aunt Rose intoned, "Leave them alone. You're going to hurt the kids' feelings, you ignorant D.P!"

Then I said, "Uncle Gino, Ted, and I are waiting until we buy a house before we have kids. I'm on the pill."

"Shh. No get-a personal, Josie," Uncle Gino whispered. "The Pope-a no like these pills."

Aunt Rose agreed with me. "It's not the Pope's business. Is he going to support a pile of kids?" Gino Jr. nodded in agreement.

"Like I said," Aunt Rose reminded, "Kids are smarter today. They plan things, not like in our day."

Dinner went ahead with a full barbecue, mostaccioli, pizza, and two desserts.

"Josie," asked Camille, "why are you basting the chicken with BBQ sauce? Here."

She promptly started basting the chicken with her pasta sauce.

"What are you doing?" I asked.

"This will taste better than that bottled barbecue stuff."

I knew they meant well, but I was unhappy. I felt I couldn't make any decisions without being preempted. My mother brought my wedding pictures and started recalling her memories of my wedding.

"Here's a picture of the DelVecchio sisters, Francie Chiaramonte, and two other heavyweights, all sitting at the same table. They ate and ate and ate and seemed so happy at the wedding."

I remembered my father, stumbling around the dance floor, drunk out of his mind. Aunt Rose was tipsy, and Uncle Gino sang, "Sorrento."

His parting words to Ted that day were, "Be-a gentile."

Ted and I opened some gifts the next day: a chafing dish, an electric blanket, a warming tray, and a fondue set.

After dinner, I realized that the pizza, mostaccioli, and tortoni were pretty much finished, and I doubted anyone other than Ted and I ate the potato salad. I never bothered to put out the apple pie as everyone seemed eager to try Aunt Camille's tortoni, which was delicious. Thus, Ted and I had lots of leftovers for the week. This was good since we both worked full time and attended night classes at the university.

My father wasn't feeling well so he was chewing garlic cloves. Mom, sitting next to him, said, "Pee-you!" as she held her nose. "Take an aspirin, will you?"

"You know last week I told Tony to make a nice dinner because I was bringing a friend of mine from work home for dinner. Tony forgot, and when I came home, all we had in the freezer were two TV dinners and 4 hot dog buns. That was our dinner. I was so embarrassed to offer that as a meal, but that's all we had!"

"Mom, did you explain to your friend that dad forgot to make dinner?" I asked.

"Of course," she replied, "but I was still embarrassed."

I had a large basil plant and asked everyone if they wanted to take some home with them.

"None for me," said my father.

"Why not?" I asked.

"Do you use fertilizer?   That's chemicals. They're no good for you."

"No, I don't put anything on my basil. It grows like a weed," I said.

"Sure," he said. "I don't believe you."

Cousin Gino intoned, "Oh, typical family fun conversation. Yuk. Yuk."

"Never you mind," continued my father.

"You kids think you know it all, but you're ruinin' the world. I went to church today…"

My mother interrupted, "because I forced you to go."

"Keep out of this," he continued. "As I was saying, I went to church today and some girl was readin' the gospel! I ain't never seen anything so ridiculous. They got women on the altar. They never did that before! And they have people shakin' hands. It's a goddam circus! And they ain't speakin' Latin anymore. Only English. That ain't religion!"

My father jumped up and went on and on. "Religion is supposed to be about 3 or 4 priests walkin' around the altar, shakin' that thing with the smoke comin' out of it."

Tony pranced around the room, waving his hand like an incense burner.

"They didn't allow no women on the altar. They don't belong there. You could even think better when the prayers were in Latin. Nobody was shakin' hands either. Pretty soon, they'll be kissin' and who knows what after that? No, I ain't shakin' no asshole's hand because he's sittin' next to me. No sir!"

"Sit down, Tony!" my mother yelled. "What's the difference anyway? You rarely go to church; I have to force you."

Rose shouted, "Sit down and give our ears a rest, will 'ya? Jesus Christ! Get me a martini, Gino."

"Tony, you-a right," said Uncle Gino. "The kids and-a women, all-a bunch-a bums!"

Gino Jr. put his head down on the table and muttered, "Here we go again."

"Hey, everyone, let's be happy. It's our anniversary!" said Ted.

Uncle Gino smiled. "You right! Let's-a sing!"

He continued, "You are my sun-a shine, my only sun-a-shine. Marriage is-a wonderful! Women are-a meez-er-able, but you no can live-a without them! Even my fat-a wife here!"

Aunt Rose objected. "I'm not fat, just chubby."

"Now-a we dance!" Uncle Gino jumped up and ran to the record player. He put on an album of Italian music and played the fastest, wildest song, "La Danza." He pulled a handkerchief out of his pocket and danced a wild, frenzied tarantella. Everyone joined in and my entire family was twirling and jumping all over my apartment.

Ted said, "I hope we aren't evicted." We weren't.

EPILOGUE

That was many decades past. Times have changed. The older family members have departed this earth, and now Gino Jr. and I and others are seniors. I guess everyone is accustomed to family oddities and behaviors. I think it all goes back to that Italian ideal – respect. I don't understand it, but it's there. It's ingrained in us. Family dinners are the same. The back-and-forth senseless disagreements are gone. The older and younger family members are on different pages, but these are normal generational differences.

As Camille once said, "It's your blood. You can never leave them."

It used to be that the older family members were more concerned with keeping their traditions, while my generation going forward is much more Americanized. Melding two cultures wasn't easy at times; we clashed, fumed, and laughed, often at the same time. Blood may be thicker than water, perhaps that's why they're still in my head and never really left.